T0370083

"I still remember the first time I was in awe of God. It came after years of attending churches and calling myself 'Christian.' It was a major turning point in my life. It is an awe of God that inspires my major life decisions as well as my daily actions. Thank you, Paul, for getting beyond symptoms and getting at the heart of the matter. This book is brilliant, and I wish every believer would read it carefully. We live in a crazy time. We need books like this to help lay healthy foundations for our lives, so that we don't spend our days overreacting to unpredictable events."

Francis Chan, *New York Times* best-selling author, *Crazy Love* and *Forgotten God*

"Paul Tripp has a way of helping us to get beyond the surface. It is clear that Paul has thought through this subject deeply. Read this book and find yourself challenged and encouraged to stand in awe of the reality of God and to take him seriously because of it!"

Eric M. Mason, Lead Pastor, Epiphany Fellowship, Philadelphia, Pennsylvania; President, Thriving; author, *Manhood Restored*

"Paul Tripp's books always challenge me and draw me closer to Christ. This book is no exception. As followers of Jesus, we can sometimes get too comfortable with God. It's easy to forget that part of knowing and loving God is revering him. If you will read this book with a hungry and humble heart, God will use it to deepen your passion for Christ as you rediscover just who God is and why we're invited to revel in his awesome glory."

Craig Groeschel, Senior Pastor, LifeChurch.tv; author, *WEIRD: Because Normal Isn't Working*

"Simply put, I read everything that Paul Tripp writes. I can't afford to miss one word."

Ann Voskamp, author, *New York Times* best seller *One Thousand Gifts*

"When you find yourself in awe of something, you never forget it. It changes you. I just finished reading this book, and I'm writing this at 2:45 a.m. in tears. Convicted—not of my sin but of my righteousness in Christ! In awe of who Jesus is and who I am in him! Tripp has tapped into something that I hope is like a defibrillator to the flatlined believer. We were made to live in awe; may we never forget this!"

Bart Millard, Lead Singer, MercyMe

AWE

Crossway Books by Paul David Tripp:

40 Days of Faith
40 Days of Grace
40 Days of Hope
40 Days of Love
Age of Opportunity
Awe
Broken-Down House
Come, Let Us Adore Him
Dangerous Calling
Do You Believe?
Forever
How People Change (with Timothy S. Lane)
Instruments in the Redeemer's Hands
Journey to the Cross
Lead
Lost in the Middle
Marriage
My Heart Cries Out
New Morning Mercies
Parenting
A Quest for More
Reactivity
Redeeming Money
Relationships (with Timothy S. Lane)
Sex in a Broken World
A Shelter in the Time of Storm
Suffering
Sunday Matters
War of Words
Whiter Than Snow

AWE

WHY IT MATTERS FOR EVERYTHING WE THINK, SAY, & DO

PAUL DAVID TRIPP

CROSSWAY®

WHEATON, ILLINOIS

Awe: Why It Matters for Everything We Think, Say, and Do

© 2015, 2025 by Paul David Tripp

Published by Crossway
      1300 Crescent Street
      Wheaton, Illinois 60187

Cover design: Tim Green, Faceout Studio

First printing 2015

Reprinted with study questions 2025

Printed in the United States of America

Hardcover ISBN: 978-1-4335-9755-8
ePub ISBN: 978-1-4335-9757-2
PDF ISBN: 978-1-4335-9756-5

Library of Congress Cataloging-in-Publication Data
Tripp, Paul David, 1950-
Awe : why it matters for everything we think, say, and do / Paul David Tripp.
    pages cm.
    Includes bibliographical references and index.
    ISBN 978-1-4335-4707-2 (hc)
    1. God (Christianity)—Worship and love. 2. Awe.
I. Title.
BV4817.T75   2015
248.4—dc23   2015003091

Crossway is a publishing ministry of Good News Publishers.

LB		35	34	33	32	31	30	29	28	27	26	25
13	12	11	10	9	8	7	6	5	4	3	2	1

To DC, Matthew, and Matt,
young friends in life and ministry.
Our gospel conversation has made me love Jesus more.

CONTENTS

PREFACE

I should start with an admission. I wrote this book for me. I am an Epicurean of sorts. I love the visual arts, I love great music, and I love food of all kinds. A beautiful, well-executed painting leaves me in awe. A band's well-constructed album leaves me amazed and wanting more. The memory of a tasting menu at a great restaurant leaves me wanting to recreate dishes and revisit the establishment. None of these things are wrong in themselves. God intended us to be in awe of his creation, but that awe cannot and should not be an end in itself.

I wrote this book for me because, at this point in my life, I am more aware than ever that I have a fickle and wandering heart. I wish I could say that every moment I enjoy some created thing initiates in me a deeper worship of the Creator, but it doesn't. Empirical evidence in my life betrays that I give my heart to the worship of the thing that has been made rather than the One who made it—spending when I don't really have a need, envying what someone else has, or eating when I'm not really that hungry.

I wrote this book for me because I am aware that I need to spend more time gazing upon the beauty of the Lord. I need to put my heart in a place where it can once again be in awe of the grandeur of God that reaches far beyond the bounds of the most expressive words in the human vocabulary. I need awe of him to recapture, refocus, and redirect my heart again and again. And

I need to remember that the war for the awe of my heart still wages inside me.

I wrote this book for me because I need to examine what kind of awe shapes my thoughts, desires, words, choices, and actions in the situations and relationships that make up my everyday life. Three years ago I lost forty pounds. That I needed to at all embarrassed me. Writing this book reminded me that my weight gain was a spiritual issue, a matter of my heart before God. Like all other forms of subtle idolatry, it didn't happen overnight. If you gain half a pound per month, you will not notice it. But that's six pounds per year, and in five years you will have put on thirty pounds. Sadly, I had to confess the sin of gluttony, put food in its proper place, and cry out for the grace to worship the Giver, not his gifts.

I wrote this book for me because I came to see that I was wired for awe, that awe of something sits at the bottom of everything I say and do. But I wasn't just wired for awe. I was wired for awe of God. No other awe satisfies the soul. No other awe can give my heart the peace, rest, and security that it seeks. I came to see that I needed to trace awe of God down to the most mundane of human decisions and activities.

I wrote this book for me, but because I did, it's a book for you as well. I know that you are like me. The war that rages in my heart rages in yours as well. Things in the creation not only capture me, they capture you too. Like me, you need to spend more time gazing upon the awesome beauty of your Lord so that your heart will remember and, in remembering, be rescued.

I wrote this book for me, but I now give it to you. May it deepen your awe of your Redeemer, and may your heart be rescued, satisfied, and glad.

Paul David Tripp
October 1, 2014

1

HUMANITY

Don't let me lose my wonder.
KEITH AND KRISTYN GETTY[1]

He was five years old, and he was enthralled by the snow. He stood on the couch watching what he thought must be the biggest blizzard ever. As he pressed his nose against the window, he thought of making the biggest snowball ever—bigger than him, bigger than his dad's car, bigger than the garage, so big that he would look like an ant next to it. The thought made him smile. Before long he was begging his mommy to let him go outside.

She was on a quest. Not just any quest. It felt like this was the most important quest of her life. Sam had actually asked her to go to the prom, and now she was on a search for a dress. But not any dress. This had to be the ultimate, most beautiful prom dress ever. As she went from store to store, she imagined the dress and the moment when Sam would pick her up and see her in that gown. He would be stunned and immediately want to spend the rest of his life with her.

He sat with the number card in his hand, listening to the all-too-rapid cadence of the auctioneer's voice at the world's most prestigious antique auto auction. He had made lots of money in his life, but he had convinced himself that he couldn't live without one more thing. It was the most beautiful automobile ever manufactured, and it would be auctioned next. As the bidding began, his chest tightened, his ears buzzed, and his hands got clammy. At the end of the day, he might be the proud owner of a gorgeous powder-blue 1965 Jaguar XKE.

When she got the call, she couldn't believe it. She rushed to the scene as fast as she could, but it was too late. The mansion of her dreams—the one she and her husband had spent twenty years of their life building and remodeling—had burned to the ground. Only ashes and smoke remained. As she got out of her car, she couldn't breathe. Things turned blurry, and the next thing she knew, she was surrounded by EMTs.

She must have dialed that radio station's number a thousand times with the hope that she would get free tickets to see the best band ever. She had all their recordings. She was a member of their fan club. She had saved up to buy a signed poster, but she had never heard them live. This was her chance. Her heart raced as a voice on the other end greeted her. It was finally going to happen. She couldn't believe it!

He was blown away. When he first entered seminary, he had no idea that this would happen. He had studied hard and done well, but this was unbelievable. It was his first Sunday. He had joined the staff of one of the biggest and most influential churches in the world. It had been his dream, and now it was coming true. He felt special, alive, and blessed.

On the one hand, it seemed stupid to pay seventy dollars for a steak. But this wasn't just any steak. No, this was a Wagyu cowboy rib eye, dry-aged over forty-five days. He just knew he would never again taste a piece of meat this quality. He didn't care what it cost. If it was the one and only time, nothing could keep him from this red-meat thrill. It was almost a spiritual experience.

He stood in line holding his mom's hand. It was going to happen. After what seemed to him like years of begging and bargaining, she had finally agreed to take him. They were in line to see the movie of his dreams, but not just on any theater screen. They were going to see the surround-sound, 3-D version on an IMAX screen. He felt he had died and gone to heaven. He held his 3-D glasses tight and couldn't wait for the wonder to begin.

It was one painting, but it may have been the most wonderful work of art a human hand had ever created. It had been touring the major galleries of the world, and she was thrilled that she would finally lay her eyes on it. She had seen it in art books and as posters but never the real thing in all its majesty. She would let nothing stop her from taking this once-in-a-lifetime opportunity.

He was bitter. He knew it was wrong, but it plagued him every day like an unwanted guest. He tried to distract himself. He tried to find joy in the people, places, and activities around him, but nothing really worked. He had been raised in a great family, and that was all he ever wanted. He had dreamed of the beautiful wife, the three sweet children, and the two-acre plot in the suburbs. He didn't want to be angry, but he was—angry at God. He hadn't asked for much. But now he was forty-five and beginning to gray. Who would want him now? He hated coming home at night. He hated being lonely. He hated his life.

The pain of the knee surgery was minor compared to the pain of what that surgery meant. Since middle school, every coach had told him the same thing: he had it—that unusual X factor that makes great athletes great. He was the star of every team he had ever played on. His ambition of becoming an NFL star with adoring fans had always seemed easily within reach. He dreamed of the day he would sign that multimillion-dollar contract. But now it was all over. That college football powerhouse would withdraw its scholarship, because, if he played again, he would never be great. It was over. His injury had killed his dream.

As the crane hoisted the sign in place, he felt as if life had been worth living. It was a rather small real-estate firm, but he had built it. He owned it. It was his. As he stood in front of his storefront, he felt like he had conquered the world. He felt he could do anything. He felt the buzz of success. And it felt so good.

He had seen them at the mall, 2013 Nike Air Jordan 1 Retros. White, red, and black—they were so cool. They were also almost two hundred dollars. How would he ever convince his parents to buy them for him? It just seemed impossible. He couldn't get the Air Jordans out of his mind. He had to find a way. He simply needed those sneakers.

He baited his hook one last time. It was getting dark, but he had to give it another try. It was out there. He had seen it before—the biggest bass in the lake. It would be the catch of his life. The fish he had already caught were just a tease. He threw his hook into the fading light one more time, and as he held onto his gear, he hoped.

What do all the people in these vignettes have in common? Awe. They get up every morning, and without ever being aware of it, they search constantly for awe. They have dissatisfaction in their souls, an emptiness they long to fill, and they are attracted to awesome things. That's why they go to great museums, stadium concerts, expensive restaurants, and play-off games. The little boy dreaming of Air Jordans is just as much an awe seeker as the successful business magnate. The teenage girl going to prom is as much on a quest for awe as the woman planning the house of her dreams. The athlete who reaches for stardom seeks the same treasure as the man who yearns for the perfect wife and family.

It's not about spiritual awareness, interest, or knowledge. It's not first about church, theology, or biblical literacy. It's not even about wanting your little life to mean something. It's something that not only believers do. It's something that every person who has ever taken a breath does. It's not bound by family, culture, history, geography, language, or ethnicity. It's not a matter of age or gender. It's not about any of these things. What all these people share in common is that they are human beings, and because they are human beings, they are hardwired for awe. And so are you.

Awe: The Helicopter View

Let's start with the big picture—the helicopter view, if you will—of this thing called *awe* that stirs deep in the heart of each one of us.

1. Awe is everyone's lifelong pursuit. She sits in her little swing with feet kicking and a big smile on her face. She doesn't know what Mommy has just given her, but it was cold and sweet, and she wants as much of it as she can get in her mouth as soon as she can get it. She is enraptured. She is in awe. For the very first time, her tongue has savored ice cream. Her little brain cannot imagine that anything in the entire world is more delightful and fulfilling than this. She is ready to live her life in pursuit of that cold, sweet wonder that the big people call *ice cream.*

He has watched the video again and again. He can't stop watching it. It's like an addiction. The music that this one performer produces all by himself is a thing of amazement. There is something about the beauty, the wonder of it all, that brings him back to the video again and again. He's seventy years old, and he has not lost one bit of his capacity for wonder.

The little girl and the old man are alike. They are on the same journey. He's just been on the road longer than she has. He has sought, pursued, invested in, savored, celebrated, and been disappointed by many, many things in his pursuit of awe. She is having her mind blown for maybe the very first time, but she will soon become an awe junkie like him. She too will spend her life in pursuit of a dream. She too will want to be amazed. The old man and the baby girl are wired the same way. Maybe neither one of them is aware of what a driving force the desire for awe is. And perhaps he will die and she will continue to live not knowing why God planted this desire in their hearts.

2. *God created an awesome world.* God intentionally loaded the world with amazing things to leave you astounded. The carefully air-conditioned termite mound in Africa, the tart crunchiness of an apple, the explosion of thunder, the beauty of an orchid, the interdependent systems of the human body, the inexhaustible pounding of the ocean waves, and thousands of other created sights, sounds, touches, and tastes—God designed all to be awesome. And he intended you to be daily amazed.

3. *God created you with an awe capacity.* We not only live in an awe-inspiring world, we've also been created with powerful awe gates so that we can take in the awe that our hearts desire. Our brains and our ears can tell the difference between beautiful music and noise. We can hear the whispered chirp of the little finch and the irritating squawk of the crow. We can see the amazing segmented sections of the well-armored beetle's body. We can see the details of color, texture, and shape. We can see moving objects without blur, and we can see very near and very far. We also feel and touch things. We feel soft, wet, hard, hot, sharp, cold, smooth, silky, and bumpy. We can taste. Our tongues know salty, sweet, sour, peppery, hot, cold, briny, rough, and creamy. We not only desire awe in our lives, we have

been wonderfully created by God with the capacity to interact with and savor awesome things.

4. *Where you look for awe will shape the direction of your life.* It just makes sense that your source of awe will control you, your decisions, and the course your story takes. If you live in awe of material things, for example, you will spend lots of money acquiring a pile of material stuff; to afford your ever-increasing pile, you will have to work a lot. You will also tend to attach your identity and inner sense of peace to material possessions, spending way too much time collecting and maintaining them. If material things are your awe source, you will neglect other things of value and won't ever be fully satisfied, because these material things just don't have the capacity to satisfy your awe-longing heart. Yes, your house will be big, your car will be luxurious, and you will be surrounded with beautiful things, but your contentment in areas that really count will be small.

5. *Awe stimulates the greatest joys and deepest sorrows in us all.* Here's a simple way to do a personal awe check. Where do you experience your biggest moments of happiness and your darkest moments of sadness? What angers you or crushes you with disappointment? What motivates you to continue or makes you feel like quitting? What do you tend to envy in the lives of others, or where does jealousy make you bitter? What makes you think your life is worth living or causes you to feel like your life is a waste? When you say, "If only I had _____," how do you fill in the blank? What are you willing to make sacrifices for, and what in your life just doesn't seem worth the effort? Look at your highest joys and deepest sorrows, and you will find where you reach for awe.

Take anger, for example. Think of how little of your anger in the last couple months had anything at all to do with the kingdom of God. You're not generally angry because things are in the way of God and his kingdom purposes. You're angry because something or someone has gotten in the way of something you crave, something you think will inspire contentment, satisfaction, or happiness in you. Your heart is desperate to be inspired, and you get mad when your pursuits are blocked. Where you look for awe will fundamentally control the thoughts and emotions of your heart in ways you normally don't even realize.

6. *Misplaced awe keeps us perennially dissatisfied.* Perhaps in ways that you have never come close to considering, your dissatisfaction is an awe problem. Perhaps it's not just that the people around you are less than perfect or your boss is hard to deal with or your children tend to give you a hard time. Maybe it's not just that you don't have the circle of friends that you've always wanted or that you've never scored that house of your dreams. Maybe it's not just that your health has declined and that old age has come too soon. Perhaps it's not just that you tend to find your mundane, everyday existence uneventful and boring. Maybe it's not just that you've never found a church where you can settle in and worship and serve. Maybe it's not just that you've found your education to be inadequate and that you've felt stuck in a career you dislike. Perhaps it's more than the fact that your neighbors are annoying and your extended family is given to too much drama. Perhaps all this dissatisfaction arises from a deeper heart dissatisfaction driven by where you have looked for awe.

7. *Every created awe is meant to point you to the Creator.* This will be a major theme of the book you have begun to read. Creation is awesome. God designed it to be awesome. And God designed you to take in creation's awesome display. You are meant to be inspired and to celebrate the awesome things that come from the Creator's hand. But as you participate and rejoice in the awesome display of creation, you must understand that

these awesome things were not intended to be ultimate. They were not made to be the stopping place and feeding station for your heart. No awesome thing in creation was meant to give you what only the Creator is able to give. Every awesome thing in creation is designed to point you to the One who alone is worthy of capturing and controlling the awe of your searching and hungry heart.

As it is true of a street sign, so it is true of every jaw-dropping, knee-weakening, silence-producing, wonder-inspiring thing in the universe. The sign is not the thing you are looking for. No, the sign points you to what you are looking for. So you can't stop at the sign, for it will never deliver what the thing it is pointing to will deliver. Created awe has a purpose; it is meant to point you to the place where the awe of your heart should rest. If awesome things in creation become your god, the God who created those things will not own your awe. Horizontal awe is meant to do one thing: stimulate vertical awe.

8. Awesome stuff never satisfies. Nothing in the entire physical, created world can give rest, peace, identity, meaning, purpose, or lasting contentment to your awe-craving heart. Looking to stuff to satisfy this internal desire is an act of personal spiritual futility. It just won't work. You would have as much success as you would if you were trying to bail water out of a boat with a strainer. The things of this world just weren't designed to do what you're asking them to do. Still, we all try every day, and when we do, we have a problem much bigger and deeper than a stuff problem. We have an awe problem.

Having It All, but Missing Awe

He was possibly the most discontented man I had ever met. In many ways he had everything that you and I could ever dream of. His successful career had gained him money, renown, and power. He had all the accoutrements of success—you know, the big house on the well-manicured property, cars in the garage, and a boat at the shore. He had a lovely wife and four grown children. He took vacations just about wherever he wanted to go. He ate at the best restaurants and joined all the right clubs. He started his own foundation to help the needy, and he attended a solid church. But the one thing he hadn't achieved was personal happiness. With all the stuff of life at his feet, he was shockingly dissatisfied and scarily driven. His wife would joke that he wanted more and that he would probably die trying to find it.

When we met, he was an unhappy man. No, that is inaccurate. He was a bitter and cynical man. He was his own archaeologist, digging back through the mound of his existence, trying to make sense of it all. He carefully examined the pottery shards of his choices and decisions. In his mind, he held up all the artifacts he had collected over the years and wondered about their true value. He leafed through pages and pages of his story—his marriage, his career, his relationship with God, his friendships, his children, and a host of other side stories. He found himself asking the one question that he thought he would never ask. He had always thought it was a question for otherworldly dreamers or losers. But the question haunted him. It greeted him in the morning and put him to bed at the end of the day. It rode with him in his car and distracted him when he went golfing. It caused him to drink more than he should and to be irritable and impatient.

He came to the point where he hated all the things he had so carefully and obsessively collected, and he really hated the fact that most people around him envied him. "If they only knew, if they only knew," was his repeated refrain. He had long since quit going to God with his angst. He felt that if God were listening, he would have helped him long ago. All that remained was to keep himself as busy as possible from early morning until late at night. Even though he was retired, he purchased a couple of small businesses—not because he needed the money but because he craved the distraction.

One of the first things he said to me was, "How could it be that I have it all and yet feel so empty?" It was a genius question, but he didn't know it. It was deeply theological, but he didn't see it. His depression kept him from understanding his own insight. It had all slipped through his fingers like bone-dry sand. He had it all, but he had come up empty. He desperately wanted me to fix it, to do something that would make it all seem worthwhile, but I couldn't.

As he talked impatiently with me, bitterness colored every word. He was crying for help, but he didn't know that the only help I had to offer, he probably wouldn't want. As he talked, in the background, these words kept crashing through my brain, "For what does it profit a man to gain the whole world and forfeit his own soul?" (Mark 8:36). He didn't have a contentment problem. He had an awe problem.

2

WAR

On the glorious splendor of your majesty,
and on your wondrous works, I will meditate.
PSALM 145:5

When you see or hear the word *war*, what comes to mind? Perhaps you think of the great world wars that changed the course of human history. Or maybe you think of the seemingly endless conflicts that plague the Middle East. Or maybe you live in the inner city and think of the gang and drug wars that turn once-safe communities into battle zones. Perhaps you think of the domestic wars that trouble marriages and families and often lead to divorce or the political wars that rob the government of its ability to secure the welfare of its citizens. All these wars are real and important, but none of them rises to the level of significance of another war that has determined the course of human history and the lives of every individual who has ever lived. What is that war? It's the war of awe, the war that is fought on the turf of every human being's heart.

Between the "already" of the sin of Adam and Eve and the "not yet" of the final redemption, a war wages over who or what will rule and control the awe capacity that God has established within the heart of every human being. As we have already seen, since every person is created with a capacity for awe, everyone is searching for a way to exercise that capacity. This awe capacity was meant to drive us to God in wonder and worship, but since sin separates us from him, our capacity for awe gets kidnapped by things other than God. So in grace, God does battle for the awe of our hearts. You could argue that one of the fundamental purposes of the great redemptive story and the person and work of Jesus is to recapture our hearts for the awe of God and God alone.

This brings us to the subject of this chapter. Because the Bible is essentially the telling of the grand redemptive story, accompanied by God's necessary explanatory notes, it also tells the story of this war of awe. Scripture brilliantly depicts for us the nature and results of what I will call in this chapter *awe wrongedness* (AWN). The biblical retelling of AWN is written for our instruction and our rescue, helping us recognize the deep danger of sin in our hearts and hunger for the rescue that only Jesus can provide. I want to trace this AWN theme throughout Scripture so you can be wise to the war that rages in your heart too.

I wish I could say that this war doesn't rage in my heart, but I can't. Sadly, AWN themes are still active in my life as well. Sometimes that means physical things rule my heart more than they should. Sometimes that means I am full of myself and act more out of pride than confidence in God. Sometimes that means I care more about the appreciations and respect of others than I do about bringing glory to God. I don't have to reflect long on my daily living to see how much the war described in this chapter and so graphically depicted in Scripture is still being fought on the battleground of my heart.

Awe Gone Wrong

It has to be without debate the saddest story ever told. Not a day in your life or mine passes without us dealing with the results of this story. This single event has made everything since harder, more dangerous, and more painful than God designed it to be. Its results bring trouble into your private life. It wreaks havoc on your marriage and relationships. It makes parenting arduous. It lies at the bottom of human conflict and global war. It makes the delight of food, money, and sex dangerous. This story captures the moment when the war of awe began.

Clearly, we can find no more powerful, graphic, and helpful portrayal of AWN than in the very moment it began in the garden of Eden as captured in Genesis 3:

> Now the serpent was more crafty than any other beast of the field that the LORD God had made.
>
> He said to the woman, "Did God actually say, 'You shall not eat of any tree in the garden'?" And the woman said to the serpent, "We may eat of the fruit of the trees in the garden, but God said, 'You shall not eat of the fruit of the tree that is in the midst of the garden, neither shall you touch it, lest you die.'" But the serpent said to the woman, "You will not surely die. For God knows that when you eat of it your eyes will be opened, and you will be like God, knowing good and evil." So when the woman saw that the tree was good for food, and that it was a delight to the eyes, and that the tree was to be desired to make one wise, she took of its fruit and ate, and she also gave some to her husband who was with her, and he ate. Then the eyes of both were opened, and they knew that they were naked. And they sewed fig leaves together and made themselves loincloths. (Gen. 3:1–7)

This is a shocking story. It is tragically true, but I'm afraid that we are so completely familiar with it that it doesn't shock us anymore. Adam and Eve had it all. Every need was supplied. There was no sin, sickness, or suffering of any kind. Everything in creation did what it was supposed to do. God was in his rightful place and willingly descended to earth to enjoy the perfect communion he had with the people he had made. Yes, there's no doubt about it: it was paradise.

But that paradise was soon to be shattered like fine china dropped on concrete. Adam and Eve were discontented with everything; they wanted more. And at the bottom of their insane quest for more was AWN. The Serpent held out to them the one thing they didn't have, shouldn't have, and could never have—God's position. He told them that all they had to do was step over God's clear boundaries, and they would become like God. This dangerous fantasy now lurks in the heart of every sinner. We want godlike recognition, godlike control, godlike power, and godlike centrality. This was the initial moment when awe of self overrode awe of God and set the agenda for every person's thoughts, desires, choices, and behavior. For billions of people ever since, awe of self has literally driven every selfish, antisocial, and immoral thing we do.

In surprising and tragic AWN, Adam and Eve ate the prohibited fruit, and the glorious *shalom* that enveloped all creation was smashed into history-altering pieces. No brain is big enough to calculate the damage that moment did. But one thing we can know for sure: at that moment, AWN was unleashed on earth and with it a war for the heart of every human being. The Bible could not comprehensively recount the true devastation of sin nor fully chronicle this war so central to the Bible's main theme—the redemptive work of the Lord Jesus Christ. So, in the midst of its central story, the Bible graphically tells and retells the story of AWN. It *is* the stain splashed on every page of God's Word.

In the unveiling of the AWN drama in Scripture, it doesn't take long for it to explode into the unthinkable—fratricide (see Gen. 4:1–16). Cain brought a sacrifice, but it was not a sacrifice of true, selfless worship of God, or else what happened next would never have occured. This story confronts us with the cruelest of ironies: one of the places where we most powerfully see AWN is in supposed acts of worship. If Cain's heart was really motivated by awe of God, then when his sacrifice was rejected, he would have grieved over it, confessed to the inadequacy of his offering, and joyfully presented a more acceptable sacrifice to God. But instead, he violently envied his brother and, in an act of jealous rage, ended his brother's life. This too is a shocking and unsettling story. It's the kind of story in the local paper that would make you sick to your stomach: brother kills brother. Cain didn't have a sibling problem, a sacrifice problem, or a religious ceremony problem. No, Cain had an awe problem, and the blood of Abel cries out as a result of his AWN.

We find a principle here, one displayed in a myriad of biblical stories: in the heart of a sinner, *awe of God is very quickly replaced by awe of self.* This *is* the great war of wars.

God's summary of this war inside humanity in Genesis 6:5–6 should send chills down your spine: "The LORD saw that the wickedness of man was great in the earth, and that every intention of the thoughts of his heart was only evil continually. And the LORD regretted that he made man on the earth, and it grieved him to his heart." It should scare you to death when you read that God is sorry or grieved for something that he created. You know immediately that this is very, very serious, to say the least. God's indictment of humanity is comprehensive and inescapably dark. Everything people think and want is wrong. Every motivation is evil. Every viewpoint and craving is tainted with iniquity. What's the bottom line here? What humans desire violates God's desires for them. The boundaries that man sets for himself go past the boundaries that God has ordained. Everything you think, desire, and say offends God because you don't care about God anymore. You don't care what pleases him. You don't care about his ownership and rulership of your life. You don't care about his holy will and his eternal glory. No, all you care about is you and what you want. Your problem is not environmental. It's not relational. No, your problem is deeply spiritual. In your God-forgetfulness, you've put yourself in the center. And the evil that has swallowed your life is but a symptom of the AWN that has swallowed your heart.

You see AWN in a completely different context in the calling of Moses. We find him in Exodus 3 as a man in exile, having fled for his life. God comes to draft him to lead the children of Israel out of Egypt, but Moses is afraid, paralytically afraid. He cannot think of taking one step toward what God is calling him to do. God meets Moses in his fear and in Exodus 4 displays to him his awesome glory. We would expect that Moses would be blown away with awe and ready to represent this awesome One before Pharaoh, but that's not what happens. At the end of God's glorious display of power, Moses begs God to send someone else. It's as if the fear of personal inadequacy and political danger has completely blinded his eyes to the awesome glory of the One sending him. Moses is not in awe of God. No, the awe capacity of his heart has been captured by fear of the Egyptians, and all he can think of is being released from the task to which God has appointed him.

Later in Moses's life, he grew in his awe of God, but the people he was leading through the wilderness were not getting it. At Mount Sinai, in a moment of miraculous divine love, God gave Moses his laws for the people he held dear. But at the very same time, the children of Israel at the base of the mountain were melting gold to create a visible idol to worship. The juxta-position between these two things is almost too much to take in. As God was on the mountain proving himself to be God, Israel was at the base of the mountain working to replace him. Again, we must note carefully the words they used. The people said of the golden calf that *they* made, "These are your gods, O Israel, who brought you up out of the land of Egypt!" (Ex. 32:4).

Is not this one of the constant, destructive, and delusional functions of AWN? AWN is all about attributing to something in physical creation—yes, even the work of your hands—what only God could do. It's failing to give praise where praise is actually due and giving praise to something that could not have produced the thing that has caused you to give praise. You will live in awe of what you credit with the blessing in your life. You will worship whatever it is that you think has produced what you celebrate. The molding and worship of the golden calf stand as powerful physical examples of awe gone horribly wrong.

Perhaps one of the clearest portrayals of AWN is what we see in the Valley of Elah in 1 Samuel 17. For forty days the army of the Most High God in fear had refused to face the giant war-rior Goliath in battle. For forty days they had listened to his vile taunt, "I defy the ranks of Israel this day. Give me a man, that we may fight together" (v. 10). Their reticence to go down into that valley and face this enemy resulted not from military posturing or tactical maneuvering. No, it resulted directly from awe amnesia. Because they failed to carry into that valley a life-shaping, courage-imparting awe of God, they based their as-sessment of the situation on a false spiritual equation. For forty days they compared their size and ability to the size and ability of Goliath and therefore concluded that he would defeat them.

David showed up to deliver a lunch to his brothers and was confused as to why the army of Israel had failed to rise to

Goliath's challenge. And then he shockingly said that he would fight Goliath. Was he that arrogant? Was he delusional? Did he not understand the impossible odds? No. Listen to what David said: "The LORD who delivered me from the paw of the lion and from the paw of the bear will deliver me from the hand of this Philistine" (v. 37). Because David was not suffering from AWN, he made the right spiritual assessment and was therefore unafraid. It was not puny little David against this awesome giant. No, it was this puny little giant against the God who is the sum and definition of all that is awesome. Now, who do you think would win? With the boldness and confidence that only the awe of God can produce, David walked into what had been for forty days a valley of fear and defeated Goliath, leading the army of Israel to rout the Philistines.

AWN causes you to feel unable, alone, unprepared, and afraid, while awe of God produces, courage, hope, and forthright action. This really is the war of wars. Too many of us, no matter what our theological persuasion, live in a functional state of AWN, and so we are timid, anxious, defeated, and struggling to hold onto the shreds of hope that we have left. Our problem is not the size or difficulty of the things we face. No, our problem is AWN and the havoc it wreaks on our daily living. AWN will cause you to fear things that you need to defeat. AWN will cause you to deny reality because you are afraid to face what is true. AWN will cause you to fret over people and situations. AWN will cause you to attempt to control what you cannot control because you think it is out of control. AWN will never lead you anywhere good.

After Genesis 3, there's no more powerful portrayal of AWN in the Bible than the story of Nebuchadnezzar in Daniel. The central theme of Daniel is the awesome and unstoppable sovereignty of God over the life of every human being and over the movement of history. You conclude your reading of Daniel assured that God really does have "the whole world in his hands." It is particularly interesting, then, that the book of Daniel also puts before us one of the Bible's most dramatic examples of AWN. The contrast between Daniel's overall theme and the story of Nebuchadnezzar should not be missed (see Daniel 3–4.)

Nebuchadnezzar had reached a height of unparalleled greatness and power. He was godlike in his own eyes and in the way that he wielded his power. So in an act of stark self-sovereignty, he created a huge golden image and commanded everyone under his power to bow down and worship his idol. It was an act of pure glory thievery. This was not about worship per se; it was AWN, that is, a leader stealing from God the awe due to him and him alone. Nebuchadnezzar reveals his AWN when he asks this rhetorical question in Daniel 4:30: "Is not this great Babylon, which I have built by my mighty power as a royal residence and for the glory of my majesty?"

Here is a king confronting the awesome glory of God with a declaration of his own glory in the form of a perverse command for all his subjects to worship an idol. This episode really captures the core of AWN. The war that rages in all our hearts is a war between the awe of God and the awe of self. The war really does somehow turn all of us into glory thieves. Perhaps we commit vertical larceny much more than we realize. Perhaps we quest for personal glory more than we think. Perhaps we take credit for what only God can do more often than we think we do. Perhaps, in subtle idolatry, we give credit to places and things when it really belongs to God. Perhaps we're not too far from Nebuchadnezzar's sin.

So in a real demonstration of his incalculable power and grace, God showed Nebuchadnezzar who was actually sovereign over all things, even over him. God brought Nebuchadnezzar low, so low that he ate grass like a bovine, reduced to animal instincts and behavior. God's goal was to deliver Nebuchadnezzar from his AWN. Listen to Nebuchadnezzar's response after the One who *is* sovereign had restored him:

> for his dominion is an everlasting dominion,
>   and his kingdom endures from generation to generation;
> all the inhabitants of the earth are accounted as nothing,
>   and he does according to his will among the host of
>   heaven
>   and among the inhabitants of the earth;
> and none can stay his hand
>   or say to him, "What have you done?" (Dan. 4:34b–35)

Nebuchadnezzar's declaration of the awesome rulership of God over a kingdom that will never end represents a confession that all of us should make daily. It would be worth printing out this confession and sticking it to the mirror that you gaze at every morning. This declaration not only reminds you of who God is but points you once again to who you are and, in so doing, protects you from the glory-stealing AWN that constantly threatens you and me this side of eternity.

The grand redemptive story, which stands as the central theme of the Bible, is dotted with portrayal after portrayal of AWN. You see it in King Saul's disobedience to God's commands to utterly destroy the Amalekite nation and everything in it (1 Samuel 15). Saul acted like he was in charge and had the right to set his own rules, and because he did, he took plunder for himself rather than destroying it all as God had commanded. To make matters worse, rather than admit his AWN-induced disobedience, he blamed the people of Israel. The prophet Samuel uncovered Saul's actual motives: "For rebellion is as the sin of divination, and presumption is as iniquity and idolatry" (v. 23). You see, Saul's problem was not that he disagreed with

God's strategy for dealing with the Amalekites. No, Saul had a heart problem. His heart was captured more by the awe of physical things than by God. AWN caused him to crave what God had forbidden and to rebel against God's clear commands. So God, in a clear display of who was in charge and who had the authority to set the rules, turned his back on Saul and his reign. AWN is not just shockingly blind and morally wrong, it is also inescapably self-destructive.

Or what of the sad theme of the book of Judges, where the people of God, who were commissioned to worship and obey the Lord and stay willingly inside his moral boundaries, again and again did what was right in their own eyes and again and again faced the consequences of doing so? Judges recounts the sad AWN cycle of disobedience, God's discipline, his gracious rescue, and more disobedience to follow.

Then there are the wayward, arrogant, and self-celebrating leaders of Israel depicted by the prophet Amos. In clear AWN, they were moved more by their own power and affluence than by the power and glory of the God they had been called to worship and serve. And because they had forgotten God, they cared little for the people whose welfare had been placed in their hands. Read Amos's description:

> Woe to those who lie on beds of ivory
> >   and stretch themselves out on their couches,
> and eat lambs from the flock
> >   and calves from the midst of the stall,
> who sing idle songs to the sound of the harp
> >   and like David invent for themselves instruments of
> >   music,
> who drink wine in bowls
> >   and anoint themselves with the finest oils,
> >   but are not grieved over the ruin of Joseph!
> >   (Amos 6:4–6)

How much of leadership today, whether in the political or ecclesiastical arenas, is shaped by leaders who suffer from AWN and are consequently more concerned about their own power and position than they are about the people they are called to lead? Maybe it's a pastor who lives outside of or above the body of Christ, as if he is essentially different from the people he leads and not one with them in both need and ministry. Or maybe it's the politician who uses his elected position more to consolidate personal power than to secure the good of those who elected him. We really do live in a leadership culture that is often not far from the AWN of the leaders in Amos's day.

Or how about the horrible New Testament story of King Herod's jealous infanticide at the time of Christ's birth? Did a more tragic and unthinkable event occur in biblical history that side of the crucifixion? Here's the brief but shocking account. "Then Herod . . . became furious, and he sent and killed all the male children in Bethlehem and in all that region who were two years old and under, according to the time that he had ascertained from the wise men" (Matt. 2:16).

The brevity of this account should not distract us from its utter and unthinkable horror. Imagine the wails of unbridled grief from distraught mothers that echoed down every street in Bethlehem and its surrounds. Could there be any worse act of AWN than this? Why did Herod do such a thing? He did it because he would not allow another king to challenge his sovereign reign. He did it because nothing held more sway over his heart than his own power and glory. He did it because he despised loss of power more than the slaughter of countless infant boys.

You could argue that every horrible act of man's inhumanity is rooted in AWN. Every moment of murder has its source in AWN. Every act of physical or sexual abuse arises from AWN.

Every moment of family violence has its roots in AWN. Every act of terrorism or needless political violence is unleashed AWN. It's AWN that makes us willing to destroy the reputation of another person. AWN causes us to respond to one another in bitterness, envy, and vengeance. AWN lies at the heart of racism and makes human culture a battleground rather than a community. When AWN rules our hearts, we harm one another.

Consider even the disciples, who were more captivated by their quest for position in the kingdom than they were grieved by the suffering and loss of their Master. After Jesus revealed his coming death and resurrection more clearly than he ever had, the very next conversation was not a discussion about the seeming impossibility of the death of the Messiah but an argument over who was or would be greatest in the kingdom (see Mark 9:30–37). The disciples had little time to contemplate the humiliation of Jesus because they were too consumed with their own greatness. Once again, these guys were not just theologically confused. No, they were trapped in the cul-de-sac of their own grandeur. They were followers of the Messiah, but they placed themselves at the center of the story. Here the agenda of the cross collided with the agenda of AWN, demonstrating how the cross was absolutely necessary.

Perhaps we can find no more powerful summary of AWN and its results than in Romans 1:

> For the wrath of God is revealed from heaven against all ungodliness and unrighteousness of men, who by their unrighteousness suppress the truth. For what can be known about God is plain to them, because God has shown it to them. For his invisible attributes, namely, his eternal power and divine nature, have been clearly perceived, ever since the creation of the world, in the things that have been made. So they are without excuse. For although they knew God, they did not

honor him as God or give thanks to him, but they became futile in their thinking, and their foolish hearts were darkened. Claiming to be wise, they became fools, and exchanged the glory of the immortal God for images resembling mortal man and birds and animals and creeping things. Therefore God gave them up in the lusts of their hearts to impurity, to the dishonoring of their bodies among themselves, because they exchanged the truth about God for a lie and worshiped and served the creature rather than the Creator, who is blessed forever! Amen. For this reason God gave them up to dishonorable passions. For their women exchanged natural relations for those that are contrary to nature; and the men likewise gave up natural relations with women and were consumed with passion for one another, men committing shameless acts with men and receiving in themselves the due penalty for their error. And since they did not see fit to acknowledge God, God gave them up to a debased mind to do what ought not to be done. They were filled with all manner of unrighteousness, evil, covetousness, malice. They are full of envy, murder, strife, deceit, maliciousness. They are gossips, slanderers, haters of God, insolent, haughty, boastful, inventors of evil, disobedient to parents, foolish, faithless, heartless, ruthless. Though they know God's righteous decree that those who practice such things deserve to die, they not only do them but give approval to those who practice them. (vv. 18–32)

This passage argues that we can in no way overstate the power and significance of AWN. It really is the battle of battles. It really is the root and source of every evil thing that we think, desire, choose, say, and do. It is the reason for all our personal, relational, and societal dysfunction. In awe wrongedness we put ourselves or the creation in the place where God alone is to be, and when we do, an endless catalog of bad things happen.

AWN is why Jesus had to come. It is the core spiritual disease from which none of us can escape. It is the war of wars
that none of us has the power to win. Why? Because that war
rages and that disease lives in our hearts. Our only hope is for
a rescuer to come and free us from ourselves. Thankfully, God,
in awesome grace, commanded the forces of nature and ruled
the events of human history so that at a certain time his Son, the
Savior, the Messiah, the Lamb, the King, would come and live
the way we should have lived and die the death we should have
died. In doing so, God made it possible for us not only to be
rescued from our AWN and accepted into his presence but also
to become people who live in moment-by-moment awe of him.

Here's the good news: God's forgiving, rescuing grace is in-
finitely more powerful than the AWN that kidnaps the heart of
every sinner. And that really is the best of news!

3

MINISTRY

He . . . who can no longer pause to wonder and stand rapt in awe, is as good as dead; his eyes are closed.
ALBERT EINSTEIN[2]

I was in ministry, but I didn't really understand it. I didn't understand ministry because I didn't understand the people I was called to serve. I didn't understand the people I was called to serve because I didn't understand life in this terribly fallen world. Sure, I said and did helpful things. I endeavored to preach the gospel of Jesus Christ to my people. I worked to counsel people with the wisdom that can only be found in God's Word, but my ministry was seriously lacking the big picture. I was doing all kinds of gospel stuff, but my ministry wasn't tied together by one central, unalterable, nonnegotiable mission. I was busy, but I didn't fully understand why.

I have met all kinds of ministry people all over the world who are just like I was. The problem is not that they're ungodly. The problem isn't that they lack pure motives. The problem isn't that they fail to do and say good things. The problem is that they lack the grand perspective, and because they do, they often lose sight of why they are doing everything they're doing.

Here's the danger: it is always easier for bad agendas to

slither their way into our hearts and into our ministries when we are unclear about the big, grand agenda that we are serving. You probably don't need me to tell you that people do ministry for all kinds of reasons other than the one grand agenda that should focus and direct every ministry activity. That was me. I didn't have the big picture, and because I didn't have the big picture, I was susceptible to being seduced by other ministry motivations. The problem was that I didn't know it.

I can't tell you how many times in my early days of ministry I questioned if God had really called me into pastoral ministry. It's embarrassing to admit how many times I decided to quit. I thought my problem was that I had been called to a difficult place. I reasoned that I had been sent to work with unusually resistant people. I envied the ministry of other people who seemed to have it better than me. I dreamed of a series of other jobs. I did a lot of moaning and complaining. I felt weak and unprepared. I knew something was wrong. I knew something was missing, but I simply had no clue what it was.

Then one day, in the mystery of God's loving and wise sovereignty, I bumped into Psalm 145, and it changed my life. No, it's not an exaggeration. It really did change me and everything about my ministry. And I have been living off those changes ever since. While I wish I could say that the battle is over for me, it's not; I've just become a more knowledgeable and committed soldier. Yet Psalm 145 gave me what I was so desperately missing: the big picture.

Ministry's Grand Agenda

I will extol you, my God and King,
    and bless your name forever and ever.
Every day I will bless you
    and praise your name forever and ever.

Great is the Lord, and greatly to be praised,
  and his greatness is unsearchable.

One generation shall commend your works to another,
  and shall declare your mighty acts.
On the glorious splendor of your majesty,
  and on your wondrous works, I will meditate.
They shall speak of the might of your awesome deeds,
  and I will declare your greatness.
They shall pour forth the fame of your abundant goodness
  and shall sing aloud of your righteousness.

The Lord is gracious and merciful,
  slow to anger and abounding in steadfast love.
The Lord is good to all,
  and his mercy is over all that he has made.

All your works shall give thanks to you, O Lord,
  and all your saints shall bless you!
They shall speak of the glory of your kingdom
  and tell of your power,
to make known to the children of man your mighty deeds,
  and the glorious splendor of your kingdom.
Your kingdom is an everlasting kingdom,
  and your dominion endures throughout all generations.

[The Lord is faithful in all his words
  and kind in all his works.]
The Lord upholds all who are falling
  and raises up all who are bowed down.
The eyes of all look to you,
  and you give them their food in due season.
You open your hand;
  you satisfy the desire of every living thing.
The Lord is righteous in all his ways
  and kind in all his works.
The Lord is near to all who call on him,

to all who call on him in truth.
He fulfills the desire of those who fear him;
    he also hears their cry and saves them.
The LORD preserves all who love him,
    but all the wicked he will destroy.

My mouth will speak the praise of the LORD,
    and let all flesh bless his holy name forever and ever.

It's all there. What I desperately needed and didn't see. It opens doors of thought, insight, and understanding. But it did more than that for me. It began to rescue me from me. Let me explain. I had read Psalm 145 many, many times. But this time, one single phrase that I had never noticed before hit me hard. I think it is the linchpin of the psalm. It's the door that leads you to what this psalm is about, what ministry is about, what life is about. I began to think that this psalm was getting my ministry where it needed to be; what was really happening was that God was getting to me. I am so thankful for that one little phrase. God used it as a tool to rescue the life of this man who had lost his ministry way.

"One generation shall commend your works to another" (v. 4). That was exactly what I needed. It immediately hit me that every moment of ministry must contribute to this goal. Whether it's the worship service, the children's lesson, the small group, or the sermon itself, each must share the central goal of holding the awesome glory of the works of the Lord before his people once again. God intends every moment of ministry to inspire awe of himself in his people. This must happen again and again and again. Why? Because we so easily become awe amnesiacs. We live between the "already"—Christ's completed and inaugurated work—and the "not yet"—the coming culmination of God's work of redemption. And since life in this period is one big war over awe, the present generation of ministry people must give the next generation their awe of God.

You don't have to look very far to see awe problems everywhere around you. Adultery is an awe problem. To the degree that you forget God's glory as the Creator of your body and his place as owner of every aspect of your physical, emotional, mental, and spiritual personhood, to that degree it is easier to use the members of your body to get whatever pleasure your heart craves. Debt is an awe problem. When your mind is blown away by the thought that God provides everything you have, that every good gift really does come from him, you are predisposed to be a good steward of the things he has provided. Obsession with the collection of possessions is the result of an awe amnesia that makes you ask of things what you will only ever get from the God of glory, who alone can satisfy your searching heart. Living for power and control is an awe problem. When you live with the rest and peace that come from keeping the power, authority, and sovereignty of God before your eyes, you don't need to work yourself into control over the people and situations in your life. Gluttony and obesity are awe problems. When you forget the glory of the satisfying grace of the Redeemer, you are susceptible to letting things like food and drink become your temporary replacement messiahs. Fear of man is an awe problem. When I forget that God's glory defines not only him but who I have become as his child, I look to people to give me meaning, purpose, and identity. The awe war is everywhere.

So I know that in ministry I will be preaching, teaching, and encouraging people who are awe forgetful, awe discouraged, awe empty, awe deceived, awe seduced, awe kidnapped, and awe weary. My job is to give them eyes to see the awesome glory of God—his glorious grace, wisdom, power, faithfulness, sovereignty, patience, kindness, mercy, and love. Further, it is my job to connect this glory to the everyday experience of the hearer in a way that engages the heart and transforms the life. Whatever the ministry moment or biblical passage being discussed, I am called to intentionally inspire awe.

Something is wrong with worship that fails to inspire awe. Something is defective in exegesis that does not inspire awe. Theological instruction that does not arouse awe is broken. Biblical literacy that fails to stimulate awe is missing something. When personal discipleship doesn't produce vertical awe, something is amiss. This is the grand agenda of every form of ministry, and once I got it, it set my ministry on a whole new trajectory—one on which it remains today.

We minister to people who are hardwired for awe, who have lost their awe, and who need awe given back to them again, so that they will not only live in awe of God but will pass that awe down to the generation that follows. Think about it. This is the job of parents, for example. You are called by God to inspire worshipful awe in your children. It is very hard for your children to get excited about God's rescuing grace and the life-directing commands of his Word if they have no awe whatsoever of the One who authored them both. You have been called to something that is profoundly deeper than being a lawgiver, a law enforcer, and a punishment deliverer. You are to exercise your authority in such a way that it gives your children eyes to see the awesome presence, power, authority, and grace of God. When our children are blown away by the glory of God, they will be predisposed to reach out for his grace and submit to his will.

The Lord's Prayer is a model for us here. The prayer that Jesus taught us to pray is an "awe prayer" before it is a "need prayer." From "Our Father" to "your will be done," the opening of this prayer presents a way of thinking, living, and approaching God inspired by awe of him. Only awe of him can define in you and me a true sense of what we actually need. So many of our prayers are self-centered grocery lists of personal cravings that have no bigger agenda than to make our lives a little more comfortable. They tend to treat God more as our personal shopper than a holy and wise Father-King. Such prayers forget God's glory and long for a greater experience of the glories of the created world. They lack fear, reverence, wonder, and worship. They're more like pulling up the divine shopping site than bowing our knees in adoration and worship. They are motivated more by awe of ourselves and our pleasures than by a heart-rattling, satisfaction-producing awe of the Redeemer to whom we are praying.

Obviously, Christ's model prayer follows the right order. And it stands not only as a model for our personal prayer but for our ministries as well. It's only when my heart is captured by the awe of God that I will view my identity rightly. And it's only when I view my identity rightly that I will have a proper sense of need and a willingness to abandon my plan for the greater and more glorious plan of God. So in ministry we work to give sight to blind eyes, to reveal the glory that so many are missing, and to inspire awe in hearts whose capacity for awe is flaccid or has been kidnapped by some horizontal awe replacement.

Ministry's Personal Protection

I've written about this before, but it is important to emphasize it here. Only a functional, heart-directed, ministry-shaping awe of God has the power to protect me from myself in ministry. It is humbling to admit, but I have had to face the fact that the greatest danger to my ministry is me! The risk is that familiarity would cause me to lose my awe. Familiarity with God's glory is a wonderful gift of grace. To be called by God to stand up close to, think about, and communicate the elements of that glory to others is a privilege beyond expression. But it is also a very dangerous thing because I very quickly replace any vacuum of awe of God in my heart with awe of myself.

I have seen it in my life and in the lives of many other people in ministry. When we replace awe of God with awe of self, we then permit ourselves to do things in ministry that no ministry person should do—to be controlling, authoritarian, self-righteous, theologically unteachable, defensive, isolated, and critical. We give way to thoughts, desires, and behaviors that are unbecoming of the gospel. We begin to think of ourselves as essentially different from the people we are called to serve. We allow ourselves to stand above the things that we teach. We begin in subtle ways to view ourselves as grace graduates. We explain away our sin and argue for our righteousness. We teach grace but are ungracious in meetings, with staff, and with our families. We approach ministry duties as a burden and not a joy. We allow ourselves to develop attitudes of bitterness and resentment against those we perceive to be our detractors. We preach and teach love, but we aren't examples of love.

Why does all this happen? The answer is simple, but it will sting you. It happens because we are full of ourselves. We have replaced awe of God with awe of self, and the harvest is not pretty. But awe of God protects you from these traps. Here's how:

1. *Your ministry is supposed to be shaped by the fear of God.* Ministry is always shaped by some kind of fear. If it is not shaped, motivated, and directed by fear of God, it will be shaped by fear of man, fear of circumstances, fear of the future, fear that you're not really called, fear of the tensions between family and ministry, or fear of financial woes. Only when the fear of God has captured my heart am I free of being dominated and paralyzed by the myriad of other ministry temptations.

2. *In ministry you are supposed to feel small, weak, and unable.* I did very well in seminary, so I graduated with a bring-

on-the-world-I'm-more-than-ready attitude. I was arrogant and self-assured. I had the mentality more of a messiah than a servant. Was I ever headed for a rude awakening! None of the people I was called to serve saw me as the messiah that I thought I was. I made just about every mistake a young pastor could make precisely because I was so scarily self-assured.

You see, awe of God will make you feel small, and that is good because that is what you and I are. Awe of God will make you feel unworthy for the task. It will confront you with a healthy inability. Not only does that sense produce a trust in God's wisdom, power, and grace, it also makes you humble, approachable, patient, kind, passionate, and willing. When you are blown away by the glory of the Savior and his cross, you will be driven to that cross for the character and strength you need to represent the Savior well in the lives of those around you. You won't be so quick to pontificate. You will be quick to admit your need. You will be obsessed not by how much people respect you, but by how much they worship their Redeemer. Fear is only ever defeated by fear. Only awe of God can ever rob horizontal awe of its power. Awe of God puts you in your place in ministry, and it will keep you there. Once you know who God is and rightly assess who you are, you will be able to minister with humility, hope, and courage.

3. *Ministry is meant to be something bigger than completing a list of tasks.* It is so easy for ministry to be reduced to a series of repetitive duties. It is so easy to lose sight of the big picture. It is easier than we think to lose sight of the awesome God we serve in the middle of days, weeks, and months of ministry busyness. It is tempting to reduce ministry to strategic planning, budget initiative, leadership development, property management, and the revolving catalog of essential meetings. And we can quickly forget why we are doing all the things we are doing.

You have been called to the high position of making the invisible glory of God visible to people who quickly lose sight of God's glory and begin to look for glories elsewhere. You could not wish to be part of something more important than this. A vision of God's glory must fuel and protect all our strategic planning. Worship, not success or an obsession with growth, must drive all our decisions about finances and property. Developing leaders is not just downloading theological knowledge and ministry skill, but calling people to lead with hearts captured by the awe of God. A person in ministry who wakes up every morning to the burdens of a job description and not to the joy of God's awesome glory is a ministry person in trouble.

4. *The spiritual warfare of ministry is all about awe.* The big ongoing battle in ministry is not a battle of time, finances, leadership, or strategy. The big battle is a battle of awe. The fear of man that grips so many ministry people and produces in them timidity and compromise is an awe problem. Sleep interrupted by anxiety about the finances of the church is an awe problem. Being too ruled and controlled by your own plan for the church is an awe problem. Being too conscious of how people see and respond to you is an awe problem. Settling for ministry mediocrity is an awe problem. Being too dominant and controlling in your ministry is an awe problem. Being self-righteous and defensive is an awe problem. Living in isolation, afraid of being known, is an awe problem. Arrogant theological "always-rightism" is an awe problem. Only awe of God can produce that balance between humility and boldness that marks all successful ministries.

5. *Awe of God is the only lens through which we can see ministry successes and hardships accurately.* Only when I look at the unavoidable hardships of daily ministry through the lens of the glory of God's sovereignty, grace, wisdom, power, faith-

fulness, mercy, and love will I ever see my ministry accurately. If I am comparing the size of my ministry difficulties to the limited resources of my wisdom, righteousness, and strength, I am making that comparison because I am a functional awe amnesiac. Here's the reality in which all ministry takes place: the God of inconceivable glory who has sent me never sends me to do his work without going with me. I am never alone in any ministry moment, never left to myself on the field of spiritual battle.

6. *Your ministry lifestyle always reveals what has captured your awe.* It really is true that a person's ministry is never shaped just by knowledge, experience, and skill but by the true condition of one's heart. In this way, all ministry ends up exposing the heart. Perhaps I am experiencing tension between my family and ministry because my heart has been captured by the awe of ministry success and, since it has, I have become a ministry workaholic. This heart condition means that, when I must choose between ministry and family, ministry will always win. Or maybe my heart has been captured by the awe of power, and the result is that I am domineering and controlling. Or it could be that my heart is captured by the respect of others, and because it is, I am tempted to compromise in places where God calls me to stand strong. Awe of something will always shape your ministry. Your ministry will only ever be protected when it is kept safe and pure by a heart-controlling awe of God and his holy glory.

7. *Finally, here's the battle, the big bad danger that lurks in the shadows of the life of every ministry person: familiarity.* Familiarity tends to blind our eyes and dull our senses. What once produced awe in us now barely gets our attention. This *is* the great danger in gospel ministry. So you must commit yourself to being humbly vigilant. You must start every day focusing the eyes of your heart on the stunning glory of God and

his amazing, life-transforming grace. You must resist allowing familiarity to replace divine glory with the ministry mundane. Yes, we all face a day-to-day battle for awe in ministry. But we are not alone. The God of awesome grace whom we serve is a God not only of past and future grace but of present grace as well. His present grace does for you what you cannot do for yourself; it rescues you from you. His grace protects you from the dullness and fickleness of your affections. His grace opens blind eyes and recaptures straying hearts. True hope for all our ministries is found in the unrelenting zeal of his right-here, right-now grace.

4

REPLACEMENT

The world will never starve for want of wonders; but only for want of wonder.

G. K. CHESTERTON[3]

It simply doesn't exist. It's humanly impossible. It would defy the way we were made. What am I talking about? Awelessness. It's impossible for a human being to live an aweless existence.

I am a new grandfather. As I held my five-month-old grand-daughter the other day, I began to think about awe and her little life. I was holding a little awe-wired, awe-inspired person. Right now, the only thing that completely captures her awe is her toes. She curls up her legs, gets her toes in her hands, and then, you guessed it, pulls her toes into her mouth—the destination of everything that gets her attention. But it won't be long before we'll see her capacity for wonder begin to shape her thoughts, desires, choices, decisions, words, and actions.

She'll develop an awe vocabulary:

"That just amazes me."
"I can't believe he did that."
"If only I had _____, then I would be _____."
"I dream about that all the time."

"It wouldn't take much to make me happy; just give me
_____."
"When I grow up, I want _____."
"I wonder what it would be like to have _____?"
"I can't believe she got what I've always wanted."
"It's so cool, I can't stop thinking about it."
"I just want to experience it once."

All people share this vocabulary because we, like my grand-daughter, are hardwired for awe. Yet this vocabulary also betrays a deeply spiritual, life-shaping, and often unnoticed principle that operates in all our lives. It is the principle of *replacement*. Every sinner quickly replaces awe of the Creator with awe of something in the creation. As the apostle Paul is discussing the sinfulness of sin and our need for rescuing grace in Romans 1, he notes that "they exchanged the truth about God for a lie and worshiped and served the creature rather than the Creator, who is blessed forever! Amen" (Rom. 1:25).

Now notice the spiritual dynamics here. The dynamics of replacement require that we buy into a devastating lie. It is the lie of lies, the lie that was first told in the garden of Eden. It is the lie that destroys countless lives, crushing them with unrealistic expectations, disappointment, anger, and hopelessness. It is the lie that leads to death. What is this powerful, dark deceit? It is the belief that life can be found somewhere outside the Creator. It is the hope that true spiritual peace, rest, contentment, satisfaction, and joy can be found somewhere in the creation. In believing that lie, Adam and Eve willfully rebelled against the position and commands of God. The Scriptures are filled with the sad stories of disobedience, violence, idolatry, greed, envy, deceit, thievery, and murder that result from believing this lie.

If human beings were created to live in heart-gripping, life-shaping awe of God—and they were—then replacing awe of

God with awe of something else will never go anywhere good. But it gets even darker and more personal, because in such replacement, we do not just generally put creation in the place of the Creator. It's more catastrophic than that. At the most foundational of heart levels, we somehow always replace awe of God in our hearts with awe of self.

Think of Adam and Eve in that moment of temptation in the garden. What was the hook? Well, it wasn't the odor and visual allure of the succulent forbidden fruit. Here's the hook as recorded in Genesis 3: "'For God knows that when you eat of it your eyes will be opened, and you will be like God, knowing good and evil.' So when the woman saw that the tree was good for food, and that it was a delight to the eyes, and that the tree was desired to make one wise, she took of its fruit and ate" (vv. 5–6). Yes, the fruit was food, and yes, it was pleasing to the eye, but what the Serpent sold—and Eve desired—was fundamentally different than a forbidden food buzz. What the Serpent offered to Eve, God's creature, was the hope that she could be in the Creator's place. She could be like him. She could have wisdom that did not depend on him. She could be at the center. She could know and experience the glory that belongs to God alone. Adam and Eve weren't just after God's forbidden fruit; they were after God's position.

This is what sin does to us all. At a deep and often unnoticed level, sin replaces worship of God with worship of self. It replaces submission with self-rule. It replaces gratitude with demands for more. It replaces faith with self-reliance. It replaces vertical joy with horizontal envy. It replaces a rest in God's sovereignty with a quest for personal control. We live for our glory. We set up our rules. We ask others to serve our agenda.

We curse whatever gets in our way. We hate having to wait. We get upset when we have to go without. We strike back when we think we have been wronged. We do all we can to satisfy our cravings. We think too much about our own pleasure. We envy those who have what we think we deserve. We pout when we think we have been overlooked. We hate suffering of any kind. We manipulate others for our own good. We attempt to work ourselves into positions of power and control. We are obsessed about what is best for us. We demand more than we serve, and we take more than we give. We long to be first and hate being last. We are all too concerned with being right, being noticed, and being affirmed. We find it easier to judge those who have offended us than to forgive them. We require life to be predictable, satisfying, and easy. We do all these things because we are full of ourselves, in awe more of ourselves than of God.

This is what Paul is talking about when he writes that Christ "died for all, that those who live might no longer live for themselves" (2 Cor. 5:15). Here we see the great replacement again. It is what sin does to us all; no longer living for God, we live for ourselves. The myriad of dysfunctions of the human community can be traced to this one thing: awe. When we replace vertical awe of God with awe of self, bad things happen in the horizontal community.

Replacement Angst

You see it played out in a thousand ways every day. If you listen, you will discover that the universal language of sinners in this broken world is complaint. When you're at the center, when you feel entitled, when your desires dominate your heart, and when it really is all about you, you will have much to complain about. It is amazing how much more natural complaint is for us than thanks or how much more we tend to grumble than we tend to praise. We talk much more about what we want than about what we have been given. Notice how much we compare what we have to what others have and how little of the time we are satisfied. Listen to people very long, and you'll hear the drone of complaint far more frequently than you'll hear the melody of thankfulness. You see, we don't first have a grumbling problem. No, we have an awe problem that results in a life of personal dissatisfaction and complaint. When awe of self replaces awe of God, praise will be rare and grumbling plentiful.

Awe lies at the bottom of a whole range of human struggles. Jim was *disappointed*. He had set his sights on that promotion for years. He had done all the right things. He had gotten to know all the right people. He had played the game well, but the promotion had gone to someone else. In his disappointment, all he could think of doing was quitting. He wasn't going to allow them to treat him this way. Now he had been out of work for eighteen months, and he didn't know what to do.

Janice was so *hurt*. She had been a loyal friend. She had had Sue's back again and again. She thought they had a bond like sisters. As an only child, she was so glad to finally have a "sibling" relationship in her life. The thought that they would be best friends forever made her smile—until Sue told her that she was moving. For six months she had known and never told Janice. When Janice found out, the room went dark. She felt she couldn't breathe, and she refused to open herself up to anyone else. After ten years, she still wondered what happened to Sue.

George was so *angry*, he wanted to punch a hole in the wall. No one was going to get away with disrespecting him like that, especially his own son. He couldn't wait for him to get home, and when he did, George would make him pay for every bit of that disrespect. "My house, my rules, and my reputation," George repeated to himself over and over again as he waited for his son to arrive.

"I could die today and no one would notice," Caleb complained.

Depressed and alone, all he wanted to do was die. "Why does nothing good happen to me? Where are all the friends I once had? What's the point? I'm forty-two with a junk job and elderly parents—nice life! I wake up in the morning and can't find a reason for living. I wish I could just turn off the breathing button."

He didn't feel like it was much to ask: "Just let my life be easy and a little predictable for once. If I had that, I'd be satisfied." Hector was so *frustrated*. It seemed to him that he had a target on his back. For every one step he moved forward, he was knocked three steps back. "I can't deal with it anymore. I just want life to work," he yelled as his frustration boiled over.

She used to love going out with Jen, but it had become increasingly difficult. They had gotten married at the same time. In fact, they had talked about having a double wedding. Whenever they were together, Jen talked about how wonderful her marriage was. But Emily's marriage hadn't produced the happiness she desired. Emily couldn't stop the *envy* she felt. Why had Jen gotten to live her dream? Emily started finding excuses for not meeting with Jen. It all seemed unfair to her.

Dan just wanted to be accepted. He longed to be part of the group of cool athletes in high school who seemed to be the center of attention wherever they went. He was all too conscious of how they responded to him, though he didn't realize that they knew it. They had the power to make or break his day. And his *fear* of never being accepted made him nervous and ill-at-ease whenever he was around them, causing him to do dumb and embarrassing things. The more he focused on their acceptance, the farther away it seemed.

John was the quintessential *loner*. He trusted no one. He was vulnerable with no one. He gave no one the chance to take advantage of him. He had been burned too many times, and it wasn't going to happen to him again. He lived with his guard up at all times. He mastered the nonanswer. He lived behind impenetrable emotional walls. He joined nothing and hung out with no one, and that was just the way he liked it. He didn't need anyone in his life but himself.

Liz was the definition of *hopeless*. She had looked everywhere for life but to no avail. She committed herself to countless activities and groups, yet they all gave her way more grief than blessing. Liz lacked motivation to do anything anymore and had to force herself out of bed each morning to go to work. She had long since given up on her church. More than once she told herself, "If life is out there, I missed it, and I am too tired to look anymore."

Eaten with anger, he determined to settle the score. Rick was filled with *vengeance*. He reasoned that nothing was more important than justice. He was determined to make wrongs right, no matter how big or small. When it came to justice, he argued, you can depend on no one else; somehow you have to make it happen yourself. And he would.

The Awe Problem in Action

At first read, the stories of these people all appear very different, but while they all differ in some ways, each of their struggles results from the same basic problem. Their core struggle is not with the people, situations, or locations of their lives. No, the disappointments with people, situations, and locations draw such emotions out of them because they all suffer from a deeper problem: an awe problem. Let me capture their struggle with some principles.

1. *Your emotional life is always a window into what has captured your awe.* It is quite clear that your emotions always reveal the true thoughts, motives, desires, longings, hopes, and

dreams of your heart. Since this is the case, it also follows that your emotional highs and lows, joys and sorrows will be connected to and flow out of what has captured your awe. If I live in a life-shaping awe of affluence, I will celebrate when financial success comes and sulk in the face of monetary loss. Only when a greater awe than the awe of physical created things has captured my heart will I be liberated from the emotional rollercoaster and live with lasting peace and rest in my heart. You see this clearly in the stories above.

2. *Awe amnesia always leads to awe replacement.* The brief vignettes above also demonstrate the principle of replacement that is the subject of this chapter. Each person has in some way, at street level, replaced awe of God with awe of something else. They have hooked the delight and satisfaction of their heart to something other than God. The problem is that they don't know it, because this seldom happens at the formal theological, confessional level. They may have a theology of awe that puts God at the center, but between Sundays they live as if God doesn't exist, hoping to be wonder-struck by an experience of some created thing. They are hurt, angry, jealous, and frustrated, not just because life hasn't worked as they wished but because awe replacement has made that disappointment a more profoundly discouraging reality for them.

3. *We replace vertical awe with horizontal addiction.* I am deeply persuaded that, much more often than we think, true worship is replaced by obsession. When my heart is enamored with the stunning glory and utter unchangeability of God, when I am living in conscious awe of him, I have no need to look vigilantly for life day after day. Vertical awe puts my heart at ease. It gives my soul rest. It produces contentment and satisfaction.

Horizontal awe is obsessive and addictive because the things to which I am looking have no ability at all to give me what

God can give. At best, the buzz of these things is short-lived, and because it is short-lived, I have to go back again and again. Because I have to go back again and again, I am looking for it all the time. And because it doesn't ever really satisfy me, I need more and more of whatever it is to give me the buzz that I am seeking. Because the physical, created world will never save me, it can never provide lasting rest of heart. As we saw, none of the people in the stories above possess hearts at rest.

4. *We quickly replace awe of God with awe of self.* Vertical awe amnesia always ends up putting me at the center. It really does make life all about me. Awe of God means I live knowing that there is a greater story than my little personal story. Awe of God means that there is a grander kingdom than my little kingdom of one. Awe of God means that God has a plan far bigger and better than any plans I have for myself. Awe of God humbles me. It puts me in my place. It reminds me that I am small, that since I am a creature of One who is far greater, it cannot be all about me.

Forgetting the awesome and glorious One who made it all and holds it all together by the sheer power of his magnificent will, will always insert me into the center. This means that no story will be more important to me than my story. I will ask no bigger question than the question of how I am doing. I will have no bigger concern than my satisfaction and comfort. I will ask life to serve me, to submit to my interests, and to deliver whatever I demand. This viewpoint will guarantee me a life of huge disappointment. And not only that, it is also an insane way to live. I am not the center of all things. The world will not do my sovereign bidding. God will not offer his awesome throne to me. Awe of self, worship of self, underlies every form of self-destructive living.

5. *Only grace can give us back our awe of God again.* The

dynamic of awe replacement, that the awe of God is very rapidly replaced by awe of self, can only drive us to one place: the cross of the Lord Jesus Christ. You see, our problem is not that we live in a world of awe-inspiring things. No, our problem is more foundationally internal and personal. Sin causes us to want for ourselves what God alone has. Sin causes us to quest for the position that belongs to him alone. Sin causes us to become all too committed to our own plans, to work all too hard to establish our own sovereignty. Sin makes us want to write our own rules and follow our own way. Sin makes us focus obsessively on how we feel, how we feel about how we feel, and how we feel about what we'll need to do to alter the way we feel. Sin makes us all God amnesiacs, and because we are, we become desperate, self-focused, unhappy, demanding, and disappointed addicts of the created world.

It's not just that we lost our spiritual minds in the fall. No, we lost a big chunk of our humanity too. No human being was meant to live this way. It is irrational and self-destructive. In fact, the Bible calls the person who lives this way a fool (see Psalm 14). The problem is that all sinners replace God with something else. It is as natural and intuitive to us as breathing. Putting ourselves in the center of our awe is the DNA of sin.

This human pattern of replacing awe of God with awe of self reminds us of how awe wrongedness has deeply twisted our hearts and our world. AWN lies at the core of all the horrible choices, family dysfunction, violence, vengeance, idolatry, jealousy, greed, immorality, foolishness, materialism, power hunger, discontentment, and self-centeredness in our world. AWN really is the hereditary and communicable plague that eats away at the heart of everyone who has ever taken a breath. No one has escaped, and no one has discovered a way to inoculate themselves. Our self-aggrandizing craziness results from this fundamental awe exchange. When we put ourselves in the center of the story, not only do we become rebels against God, we become a danger to ourselves and others. And since we are our greatest problem, we are left powerless to help ourselves.

To push further, if this universal awe replacement is our problem, then it is the height of theological absurdity to think that the law can deliver us. What set of rules can decimate our bondage to ourselves or our tendency to put the creation where only the Creator should be? What set of laws can return our wonder, amazement, worship, and awe? The law can reveal how much you have put yourself in the center of the story, but it has no power to put God back in his rightful place in your heart. We are confronted with the utter foolishness of repeatedly asking the law to do what only grace can accomplish.

No human solution can fix our replacement instincts and our replacement lifestyle. No set of rules will free us. No social or political insights will liberate us. We have met the enemy, and it is us, and because it is, we have no power to defeat it. We *will* forget God. We *will* replace him with something else. We *will* place ourselves at the center. And thus, we *will* live driven and dissatisfied lives, self-centered and immoral in the deepest sense of both terms. And we *will* live as a danger to ourselves and others, because only when God is in his rightful place will we set ourselves and others in the appropriate place in our hearts.

This is why Jesus had to come. The law was not enough. The revealed theology of the Scriptures was not enough. Kings, judges, and prophets were not enough. We needed a means by which God could forgive us for our awe thievery and a means by which God could free us from our self-slavery. And this means had to be exercised without compromising God's holy position and justice. That means was the Lord Jesus Christ. He came and lived perfectly so he could go to the cross as the

spotless Lamb. He died willingly, satisfying God's just require-
ment. He rose again, defeating the power of sin and death over
us. And part of why Christ did all this was to give us back our
awe, so that we would live for him once again and celebrate his
awesome glory, not just now but forever and ever.

So we have only one place of hope, one solid rock on which
to stand, and that rock is Christ Jesus. Only when we admit that
we have awe-fickle hearts will we begin to reach out for and
cling to the forgiving, transforming, rescuing, and delivering
grace of Jesus. To the degree that we deny the awe wandering of
our hearts, to that degree we devalue the grace that is our only
hope in life and death.

When you humbly accept the very bad news of our awe replacement, you will then seek and celebrate the very good news
of God's grace. Because of Christ's work, that grace is yours for
the taking.

5

AMNESIA

There is not one little blade of grass, there is no color in this world that is not intended to make men rejoice.
JOHN CALVIN[4]

It is the worst kind of blindness. It's the physical ability to see without the spiritual ability to really see what you've seen. It's the capacity to look at wonders, things specifically designed to move you and produce in you breathless amazement, and not be moved by them anymore. It's the sad state of yawning in the face of glory.

I remember taking my youngest son to one of the national art galleries in Washington, DC. As we made our approach, I was so excited about what we were going to see. He was decidedly unexcited. But I just knew that, once we were inside, he would have his mind blown and would thank me for what I had done for him that day. As it turned out, his mind wasn't blown; it wasn't even activated. I saw things of such stunning beauty that brought me to the edge of tears. He yawned, moaned, and complained his way through gallery after gallery. With every new gallery, I was enthralled, but each time we walked into a new art space, he begged me to leave. He was surrounded by glory but saw none of it. He stood in the middle of wonders but was bored out of his mind. His eyes worked well, but his heart was stone blind. He saw everything, but he saw nothing.

Sadly, many of us live this way every day even though God has designed the world in which we live to be a *gloryscope*. What does this term mean? Just as a telescope points you to the stars and magnifies them for you to see their illuminating glory, so the earth focuses our eyes on God and magnifies his glory, so it can produce wonder in us. Every beautiful and amazing sight, sound, color, texture, taste, and touch of the created world has gloryscopic intention built into it. Every powerful and mighty thing, animate and inanimate, is gloryscopic by design. No created beauty is an end in itself. No physical wonder exists in isolation. Nothing that is, just is. Everything exists for a grand, vertical purpose.

The glories of the physical world don't reflect God's glory by happenchance. No, God specifically and carefully designed the physical world to reflect him, that is, to be the gloryscope that our poorly seeing eyes so desperately need. As the technician grinds the lens of the telescope for the best clarity and magnification possible, so God fashioned his world in such a way that it would bring his glory into view. God created every fish, stone, flower, bird, cloud, tree, monkey, and leaf to be gloryscopic because our loving Creator knows how fundamentally blind we can be.

Pay attention to what these passages say about the way God designed the created world to function:

> The heavens declare the glory of God,
>   and the sky above proclaims his handiwork.
> Day to day pours out speech.
>   and night to night reveals knowledge.
> There is no speech, nor are there words,
>   whose voice is not heard.

Their voice goes out though all the earth,
  and their words to the end of the world. (Ps. 19:1–4)

Holy, holy, holy is the LORD of hosts;
the whole earth is full of his glory! (Isa. 6:3)

For what can be known about God is plain to them, because
God has shown it to them. For his invisible attributes, namely,
his eternal power and divine nature, have been clearly per-
ceived, ever since the creation of the world, in the things that
have been made. (Rom. 1:19, 20)

We can also be so incredibly forgetful. We learn things that
soon become distant memories, having little effect on the way
that we think about ourselves and live our lives. People do wonderful things for us, but we forget their kindness so quickly that
we even fail to e-mail them a simple "thank you." We learn
things about our family heritage, things that explain who we
are and why we do what we do, but we soon fail to recall this
history and ask the same questions of ourselves that had previ-
ously been answered. We forget old friends. Events of the past
fade from memory. The concerns of the present so dominate
our minds that we have little mental energy left to remember
what came before. In fact, many of us have totally forgotten
an incredible identity-giving story that defines not only us but
everything about life. So we live wandering, disjointed lives,
or we work to be the authors of our story, trying to make our
personal narrative turn in the direction we would like it to turn.
And in so doing, we attempt what we cannot do and want what
we will never get.

Because of our forgetfulness, God has created the physical
world to be *mnemonic*, to help us daily remember that we are
not alone, that we are not at the center, that life is not primarily
about us, and that there is a grander story than the little stories

of our individual lives. Physical things are meant to remind us of the grandeur and glory of the One who created all those things, set them in motion, and keeps them together by the awesome power of his will. These constant little physical reminders don't just happen either. God has carefully planted them in creation to protect us from our amnesia.

The earthly father is a God-given mnemonic device to remind us of the glory of the heavenly Father. The shepherd is a mnemonic device to remind us of God's care for his own. The snow is meant to remind us of the Lord's purity and holiness. The storm is a mnemonic device to remind us of God's power and wrath. The daily rising sun is a mnemonic device to remind us of God's faithfulness. We're literally surrounded by gracious reminders of the presence, power, authority, and character of God because he designed created things to function mnemonically. He knows how quickly and easily we forget and how vital it is for us to remember, so he embedded reminders everywhere we look in his creation.

But even with all that, we still tend to be blind and forgetful. When *blindness* combines with *amnesia*, nothing good results, yet that's just what sin does to us. It blinds our eyes and dulls our hearts. We all carry the corrupted capacity to look at the world around us and miss God. We enjoy the glories of creation, yet as we do, we fail to remember the Creator. God meant the earth to ignite and stimulate awe in us. As we encounter the physical world every day, we should be blown away by the glory of God to which it points. But we're not.

In fact, many of us are positively bored and uninspired. We have every reason to be stunned by God's glory, to live in life-shaping awe of him. But at street level, we tend to live as *blind amnesiacs*, and most of us don't even know it. We think that we see quite well, and we think that we remember what is important, but we don't. In our blindness and amnesia, we lose our vertical awe, and so our capacity for awe gets kidnapped by other things. I want to examine with you the symptoms of our amnesiac living and then consider what kind of help we need and where we can find it.

Our Blind Amnesia

So what are the symptoms of our blind amnesia? Here is a suggested, though not exhaustive, list:

1. *Self-centeredness.* This is something I have written about a lot. You see it in the crankiness of the baby, the rebellion of the little boy, the entitlement of the teenager, the demands of the young bride, and the grumbling of the old man. If you're not living in awe of God, you are left with no higher agenda than to live for yourself. It really does get reduced to your wants, your needs, and your feelings. You really do become obsessed with your own happiness. You really will see other people as standing in your way. Dysfunction will color every aspect of your life because you are in a place where you were never created to be: the center of it all. *When do you tend to get angry because life hasn't worked according to your plan?*

2. *Entitlement.* If life has ceased to be about God and therefore has become all about you, then you will tend to live a lifestyle driven by the language of "I deserve ____" or "I have a right to ____." To live in awe of God means that you are motivated by his will and his honor. When that awe is missing, you will live in pursuit of what you think you need, deserve, or have a right to. And here's how this operates. Once you think you're entitled to it, you will think it's your right to demand it, and you will judge the love of God and the people in your life by their willingness to deliver it. So, much of our anger with one another and our disappointment with God results from an

aweless mentality that produces an entitled way of living. *Where do you tend to give in to an "I deserve ____" way of living?*

3. Discontent. If awe amnesia has put you in the center of your world, convincing you that you are entitled to things that you're not really entitled to, you will always struggle with discontentment. The people in your life aren't in your life for the sole purpose of making you content and happy. The world around you wasn't designed to do your bidding. Life simply won't operate according to your personal plan. Things don't stop and start based on your whims and wishes. True and lasting contentment always results from living for something bigger than yourself. Sturdy contentment that can weather the storms of difficulty and want is always rooted in worship. When the most motivating pleasure in my life is the pleasure of God, I will be content even in circumstances that would tend to make us all grumble and complain. We tend to be way too discontent way too much of the time, not because we have a need problem but because we have an awe problem. *Be honest right here, right now: do you live a content lifestyle?*

4. Relational dysfunction. We all experience nastiness, criticism, hurt, anger, disappointment, vengeance, and bitterness in some way in the relationships in our lives, and so much of it is connected to and produced by our awe amnesia. Because we do not functionally connect our lives, meaning, hopes, joy, identity, and satisfaction to the awesome glory of God, we look to other people to do for us what they have no ability to do. We want our children to give us identity, and we ask our spouses to be our personal saviors. We want our friends to make us feel good about ourselves and our bosses to give us a reason to get up in the morning. Because awe of God isn't filling our hearts, we put people where God should be, and because we put people in a position they were never designed to fill, they always disappoint us. So we expect and demand and get hurt and disillusioned. We get angry and strike back and find ourselves in a seemingly endless cycle of unrealistic expectation and relational disappointment. Only when God takes his rightful place in our hearts will the people near us stand in the appropriate place in our lives. *In what ways do you ask things of people that they will never be able to deliver?*

5. *Control.* One of the most awesome and glorious things that the Bible says about God is that he rules over all things. Acts 17:24–28 even says that he determines the exact location where each of us will live and the exact span of our lives. Hold on to your hat. God does this for every person living, every person who has ever lived, and every person who will live! To say that God is sovereign means that no situation, location, and relationship that you and I will ever find ourselves in is outside of his wise and careful rule. He was ruling before the origin of this world, and he will rule after this world as we know it is gone. You and I are meant to be mystified, blown away, and left in silent, worshipful amazement in the face of his unshakable eternal sovereignty over everything that exists.

But functional vertical amnesia will rob you of your rest in God's control and cause you to want to take control. You will tend to want too much power and to be too trusting of your own wisdom. You won't rest in the fact that God's will will be done; you will try to exert your own will over people, places, and things. You will try to control what you have little power to control, will experience frustration over your lack of control, and will be intimidated by people who try to control you. You see, you struggle with control not primarily because you have a control problem but because you have an awe problem. *Where do you fear your lack of control or try to take control of things that you can't actually control?*

6. *Fear.* As mentioned earlier, the only thing that has the power to defeat fear is fear. Only when the grander fear of God rules your heart will you be free of all the little fears in life that chip away at your heart. When you live in a reverential awe of the magnitude of God's power and authority and are stunned by the fact that he exercises his power for his glory *and* your good, then you can be free from all the anxieties that make you timid and rob you of joy.

I think that we are motivated by fear, worry, dread, and anxiety much more than we realize. The decisions we make and the actions we take are motivated more often by avoiding what we fear than by the courage of faith. Courage results not from trusting yourself, other people, or your circumstances. All these things will fail you. Courage results from being in awe of the majesty of God, that worshipful fear that grips your heart when you are confronted with his holy grandeur. Because you are in awe of who God is and because you know that this awesome One is in you, with you, and for you, you do not live in fear of people, locations, and situations. *Where do you see fear setting the agenda for the way that you respond to the people and situations in your life?*

7. *Anger.* When I began to counsel on a regular basis, the one thing that surprised me was how many of the people I counseled were angry with God. They didn't know that they were angry with God, and it was not the thing that caused them to seek help, but when they began to talk about God, they described a "God" I didn't know. They described a "God" who was different from the God of the Bible. The "God" they described was distant, uncaring, capricious, unfaithful, judgmental, and angry. Their "God" lacked love, mercy and, grace.

At first, I thought my counselees had a theological problem. I thought they had been poorly taught. But as I listened more carefully, I realized that their anger problem was not first a formal theology problem; it was an awe problem. These were people who had lost their awe and so had inserted themselves in the middle of their own little world, and they were mad that God hadn't come through for them. They were mad that life had been hard in places. They were mad that the people around them were less than perfect. They were mad that their bodies didn't always work and that the world around them didn't function very well. Their view of God's goodness was directly attached to their own experience of happiness. They didn't see God as a Lord of awesome glory; in their functional theology, they had reduced him to a divine concierge. His job was to make sure that all their days were good days. He was the divine waiter, delivering the good life to them on his divine platter.

Here's the reality: most people who are angry with God are angry with him for being God. They're not angry because he has failed to deliver what *he* promised. They're angry because he has failed to deliver what *they* have craved, expected, or demanded. When awe of self replaces awe of God, God ceases to be your Lord and is reduced to being your indentured servant. *What in your life would cause you to struggle with anger toward God?*

8. *Envy.* Think with me for a moment. What is the cause of envy? Envy is not a need problem, it's not an inequality problem, and it's surely not a partiality-of-God problem. Envy is an awe problem. When I am in awe of God's greatness, when I am stunned by his holy justice and mercy, and when I am blown away by the thought that all the Lord's ways are right and true, I am able to live a grateful and content life. But when my capacity for awe has shrunk to the size of my desires or to the size of the glories of the created world, I will become a scorekeeper. I will always be comparing what I am, have, and have experienced to my neighbor. I will struggle with the blessing that others enjoy.

I will struggle to be satisfied, and I will forever be plagued by the question of why others enjoy what I have never had. *Where is envy a regular struggle of heart for you?*

9. *Drivenness.* Awe and rest are foundationally connected. I am to live with the grand thought that God rules over all things for the sake of his children, that he has made a covenantal promise to meet every one of our needs, and that he is the ultimate definition of everything that is good, right, wise, and true. When I do, I won't load the world on my shoulders. God has called me to work, but he has promised to provide. God has called me to parent my children wisely, but only he can build character in their hearts and even cause them to believe. God has called me to be a good steward of what he has provided, but he controls all the outside forces that I must interact with as I do this. Perhaps drivenness arises more from self-glory than we tend to think. When the grandeur of God is not in our eyes and filling our hearts, we will live as if it is all up to us, always working more and trying harder. Awe permits you to enjoy Sabbaths of rest. *Is your schedule too full, or are you working too much and too hard?*

10. *Exhaustion.* Living with atrophied awe is an exhausting way to live. All the things that we have considered in this list of awe amnesia symptoms will leave you weary and wanting to get off the never-ending treadmill. I have met and continue to meet so many exhausted Christians, and as I have listened to their stories, I have concluded that they don't first have a demanding schedule or busyness problem; what they have is an awe problem. Let me say it this way: they have a glory and grace problem. If you lose sight of God's incalculable glory, you will live like a king instead of trusting the King, and you will load kingly burdens on your shoulders. If you lose sight of God's amazing grace, you will try to produce by human effort what

will only ever come by means of divine grace. You will work harder because you will always feel you need to work harder or do better, and you will exhaust yourself in the process. *Be honest: does your way of thinking about and living life exhaust you?*

11. *Doubt.* Ironically, awe amnesia is the principal producer of doubt of God. Here's how it works. The more you lose sight of the centrality of God's awesome presence and grandeur, the more you will focus on yourself. The more you focus on yourself, the more you will focus on your wants, needs, dreams, desires, hopes, goals, expectations, and feelings. The more you focus on these things, the more you will define the love of God by his willingness to deliver them. And as God continues to deliver what he's promised but does not give you what you want, you will begin to doubt his goodness and his love. This cycle devastates people's spiritual lives because when you doubt God's love, you cease trusting him and thus quit going to him for help. *Where is there evidence of doubting God in your life?*

12. *Spiritual coldness.* I had a counselee say it to me clearly, "I can't go to church and sing 'Great Is Thy Faithfulness' anymore because, frankly, Paul, I just don't believe it anymore." She had quit going to her small group. She had quit coming to services on Sunday morning. She had stopped reading her Bible. She was spiritually cold and bitter. Meanwhile, God was still doing, in glorious grace, everything he had promised to do in her and for her. He had not forsaken his wise and holy plan in order to become a servant of what she was convinced she needed. It seems blatantly obvious to say, but there is a direct connection between awe and worship. As I have already stated, we quickly fill the vacuum where awe of God was with awe of self, and when we do, heartfelt worship dies. *Do you find joy in the daily worship of God? If not, why not?*

Awe Amnesia = Spiritual Anorexia

So here's the bottom line. When you are blind to the stunning, expansive glory of God, when you fail to remember his infinite greatness, you will live with an atrophied heart. Rather than your view of life continuing to expand to the size of God's incomprehensible grandeur, your perspective on life will shrink to the size of personal hopes and dreams or to the size of what the surrounding physical world has to offer. You will eat little of the true and satisfying food of God's glory, and you will try to feed yourself on the nonnutritive morsels of the temporary glories of creation. Because you won't be getting proper spiritual nutrition, you will be constantly hungry, your spiritual muscles will shrink, and you will be unable to live as God intended.

I would like to give you a set of directions to fix all this, but I just don't think it's that simple. We must begin by confessing that we have cold, fickle, and often selfish hearts. We must begin by admitting that, although God made the physical world around us gloryscopic and mnemonic, we often see and remember little of what the world points us to. We get so obsessed with our own desires, plans, schedules, and accomplishments that we have little time for meditative reflection on the awesome glory that is ours to see and remember. We have lost our wonder and, in so doing, have shrunk our souls to the size of momentary, earthbound hopes and dreams. Because we have, we get disappointed, mad, and envious too quickly.

Perhaps we don't need to institute another reformation program for ourselves. Or give ourselves to a new set of commitments that are more about penance than repentance. Perhaps what we need to do is fall down on our knees before the Great Physician in humility, brokenness, and grief and confess the awe amnesia that eats away at our hearts like a spiritual cancer. Today, plead for eyes to see and a heart that remembers. Today, mourn how easy it is for you to forget God. Confess your spiritual anorexia, and cry out for a changed heart. When you and I begin to confess that we are the problem, we can run nowhere but to God's arms of grace.

As I have written many times, you can run from a situation, you can run from a relationship, and you can run from a location, but you cannot run from you. When you confess that your problem is internal, not external, you only have one rock to stand on, and that rock is Jesus Christ. You don't have to live in some form of spiritual shame. Jesus didn't come, live, die, and rise again to shame you. No, he did all these things to redeem you. Your admission of awe amnesia is a confession of your continuing need of your loving Redeemer. Awe amnesiac that you may be, run to him and see what he will do through his incomparable, efficacious grace.

6

TRANSGRESSION

If every moment is sacred and if you are amazed and in awe most of the time when you find yourself breathing and not crazy, then you are in a state of constant thankfulness, worship and humility.

BERNICE JOHNSON REAGON[5]

He was just nine months old, but he knew good and well what he was doing. He had begun to walk, opening the doors to a whole new world of danger. I had toddled him over to the electric wall socket and lectured him on its risk. I told him never to touch it and never to put anything into it. I had no idea if we were communicating or not.

The next day, I heard the *pitter-patter* of his feet coming down the hallway as I read the paper. He peeked around the corner to see if I was looking, made a beeline for the electric outlet, and, just before he reached out to touch it, glanced back at me again. That look back was a *hermeneutical* moment. It told me that this little boy knew not only that he was doing something he shouldn't do but that it was against me. He was acting in violation of what his loving father had warned him about. In that moment, he was willing to break relationship with me in order to experience something that, out of love for him, I had forbidden. This little moment revealed not just a moral struggle but something deeply personal as well.

Remembering that moment with my toddler son reminded me of another moment, dramatically different on the surface but very similar at the core. It was an awesome, mind-blowing, heart-quaking, fear-inducing transitional moment. There had never been a situation like this before. It was designed for one very special group of people, so that they would never be the same again. When you read the account of this moment, you sense that the words cannot even capture its thunderous majesty. God chose one man to stand closer to him than any man had since the disaster in the garden of Eden. And this man was to receive from the hand of God what God had never given before. Surrounded by God's glory, he received God's law, written on tablets of stone.

Although the Mosaic law set conditions for the people to continue enjoying God's blessing, it wasn't primarily given as an achievement test, a list of things that this special group of people had to do to gain acceptance and relationship with God. No, God had already chosen them. He had already placed his love on them. He had already redeemed them from captivity. He had already promised them a land and a future. The law he had given was not a test to gain his love; rather, it was a concrete expression of his love. God was gracing the people whom he had taken as his own with his law. That they were chosen to receive it depicted the special nature of their relationship with him—a relationship that other nations did not enjoy.

So this meant that when they disobeyed, they did something profoundly more significant than break abstract moral regulations. Disobedience was personal. Breaking law was breaking relationship. Turning their backs on God's moral code was turning their backs on God. Rebellion was more than transgressing legal boundaries; it was disloyalty to God.

The same is true for us. We have by grace become a people for God's own possession. God has welcomed us into eternal communion with him, which we could never have achieved by our own righteousness. On our very best moral day, we fall dramatically below God's holy standard. We are his only because of lavish mercy and incalculable love. To disobey, then, is spiritual adultery, giving the affection that belongs to God to something or someone else. Transgressing God's boundaries or breaking his law is first about breaking relationship with him.

"What does the law have to do with a book on the awe of God?" you may be asking at this point. Well, I am more and more persuaded as I read Scripture that transgression is not first a law problem; rather, an awe problem produces a law problem. When awe of anything but God kidnaps and controls your heart, you simply will not stay inside God's boundaries. But when a deep, reverential fear of God has captivated your heart, you will willingly and joyfully live inside the fences he has set for you. When the glory of some created thing rules your heart, you will live not for the glory of your Redeemer but for that thing. When love for a certain thing is a more dominant motivator than love for God, you will turn your back on God, and as you do, you will step over his boundaries.

The seedbed for a life of obedience is awe. When awe of something other than God replaces awe of God, disobedience will replace obedience. A life of submission to God's will, plan, commands, and purposes flows out of the worship of the One who has given those commands. Obedience is not the impersonal following of a set of arbitrary and abstract laws. Obedience is being in such awe of God that you are blown away by his wisdom, power, love, and grace, which makes you willing to do whatever he says is right and best. Obedience is deeply more than begrudging duty. It is a response of joyful willingness ignited by, stimulated by, and continued by a heart that has been captured by God's glory, goodness, and grace.

Thus, you cannot threaten, manipulate, or guilt a person into obedience. Only grace can produce this joyful submission in me. Only grace can open my blind eyes to the awesome glory of God. Only grace can free my heart from all the replacement awes that have kidnapped me. Only grace can give me back my awe of God. Only grace can transform me from a worshiper of self to a worshiper of God. Only grace can motivate me to gaze upon the beauty of the Lord until I have exited my little government of one and given myself to the work of something vastly bigger than me. The law cannot motivate me to keep the law.

So, in our disobedience, we don't first have a law problem; we have an awe problem. Awe of God will produce willing submission to his will, and a lack of awe of God will lead me to step over his boundaries. I want to examine this theme by unpacking three familiar portions of Scripture.

The Awe Exchange in the Garden

Now the serpent was more crafty than any other beast of the field that the LORD God had made.

He said to the woman, "Did God actually say, 'You shall not eat of any tree in the garden'?" And the woman said to the serpent, "We may eat of the fruit of the trees in the garden, but God said, 'You shall not eat of the fruit of the tree that is in the midst of the garden, neither shall you touch it, lest you die.'" But the serpent said to the woman, "You will not surely die. For God knows that when you eat of it your eyes will be opened, and you will be like God, knowing good and evil." So when the woman saw that the tree was good for food, and that it was a delight to the eyes, and that the tree was to be desired to make one wise, she took of its fruit and ate, and she also gave some to her husband who was with her, and he ate. Then the eyes of both were opened, and they knew that they were naked. And they sewed fig leaves together and made themselves loincloths.

And they heard the sound of the LORD God walking in the garden in the cool of the day, and the man and his wife hid themselves from the presence of the LORD God among the trees of the garden. But the LORD God called to the man and said to him, "Where are you?" And he said, "I heard the sound of you in the garden, and I was afraid, because I was naked, and I hid myself." He said, "Who told you that you were naked? Have you eaten of the tree of which I commanded you not to eat?" The man said, "The woman whom you gave to be with me, she gave me fruit of the tree, and I ate." Then the LORD God said to the woman, "What is this that you have done?" The woman said, "The serpent deceived me, and I ate." (Gen. 3:1–13)

Although we examined this passage earlier, I want to remind us again of just how shocking it was for Adam and Eve to disobey God and why they did. You have to examine the words carefully here to get the full import of the nature of Adam and Eve's disobedience. Let me set the stage by helping you consider the miraculous, awe-inspiring scene that they enjoyed daily in the garden. The passage tells us that after Adam and Eve had disobeyed God and were hiding from him, they heard the sound of him "walking in the garden in the cool of the day" (v. 8). What? Let your imagination take in the amazing reality that these words portray. In condescending mercy, God, who from all eternity had existed as a spirit, took on some kind of seeable and hearable physical form so as to have regular, loving community with the people that he had made. God didn't require Adam and Eve to reach up to him; he came down to them, incarnating himself in some way to make himself physically relatable to them.

This is the Lord of lords, the eternal sovereign One, the Creator of all that exists, inviting human beings into fellowship with him and doing miraculous things to make their fellowship possible. How could anything more awe-inspiring occur in Adam and Eve's lives? How could they experience anything more glorious than this? How could they not be blown away by their day-to-day fellowship with God? How could this not leave them in wonder and amazement? The moment you begin to understand the miraculously close communion that Adam and Eve enjoyed by God's grace, you begin to understand that their disobedience was more than a technical breaking of abstract regulations; their disobedience was fundamentally personal.

Now what is the Serpent trying to sell to Eve? He is trying to convince her of the constructive power of disobedience. This is what temptation always does. It tells you that if you step over God's boundaries, good stuff will be built into your life. The Serpent is arguing for the constructive power of what is actually destructive because he is working to create an awe shift in Eve. He is trying to get her imagination to run wild, to consider what it would be like not to have to live in a subservient relationship to God anymore. He's doing this so that her heart would be motivated more by the glory of the vision that he is holding out to her than by her awe of the glory of God and her special position as the object of his love. When awe of what could be replaces awe of God, Eve steps over God's fences and eats what is forbidden. Eve doesn't first have a law problem; she has an awe problem that produces a law problem.

But there is something else to observe that reinforces what we have already said. The passage notes that Eve saw that the tree was "to be desired to make one wise" (v. 6). Now let this sink in: "to be desired to make one wise." Eve was enjoying close, personal, loving, daily communion with the One who is Wisdom. She was in fellowship with the most awesome source of wisdom that ever existed or ever would exist. She didn't need wisdom. The garden wasn't a place of wisdom famine. So what then was Eve seeking? What kind of wisdom vision captured her awe? The Serpent was selling Eve *autonomous* wisdom, that is, wisdom that would no longer depend on God as its source. Instead of awe of God producing in her a submission to his wise will, awe of independent wisdom caused her to rebel against God's will.

In the garden that day, a great and destructive exchange took place—not first an exchange of obedience for disobedience but awe of God for awe of self. It was a look-what-you-could-be form of temptation that aggrandized Eve and made God seem small. Once awe of God is lost, the loss of a heart to obey isn't far off.

Spiritual Adultery

I made my vow to you and entered into a covenant with you, declares the Lord GOD, and you became mine. Then I bathed you with water and washed off your blood from you and anointed you with oil. I clothed you also with embroidered cloth and shod you with fine leather. I wrapped you in fine linen and covered you with silk. And I adorned you with ornaments and put bracelets on your wrists and a chain on your neck. And I put a ring on your nose and earrings in your ears and a beautiful crown on your head. Thus you were adorned with gold and silver, and your clothing was of fine linen and silk and embroidered cloth. You ate fine flour and honey and oil. You grew exceedingly beautiful and advanced to royalty. And your renown went forth among the nations because of your beauty, for it was perfect through the splendor that I had bestowed on you, declares the Lord GOD.

But you trusted in your beauty and played the whore because of your renown and lavished your whorings on any passerby; your beauty became his. You took some of your garments and made for yourself colorful shrines, and on them played the whore. The like has never been, nor ever shall be. You also took your beautiful jewels of my gold and of my silver, which I had given you, and made for yourself images of men, and with them played the whore. And you took your embroidered garments to cover them, and set my oil and my incense before them. . . .

And after all your wickedness (woe, woe to you! declares the Lord GOD), you built yourself a vaulted chamber and made yourself a lofty place in every square. At the head of every street you built your lofty place and made your beauty an abomination, offering yourself to any passerby and multiplying your whoring. You also played the whore with the Egyptians, your lustful neighbors, multiplying your whoring, to provoke me to anger. Behold, therefore, I stretched out my hand against you and diminished your allotted portion and delivered you to the greed of your enemies, the daughters of the Philistines, who were ashamed of your lewd behavior. You played the whore also with the Assyrians, because you were not satisfied; yes, you played the whore with them, and still you were not satisfied. You multiplied your whoring also with the trading land of Chaldea, and even with this you were not satisfied. . . .

Men give gifts to all prostitutes, but you gave your gifts to all your lovers, bribing them to come to you from every side with your whorings. So you were different from other women in your whorings. No one solicited you to play the whore, and you gave payment, while no payment was given to you; therefore you were different. (Ezek. 16:8b–18, 23–29, 33–34)

The language is shocking, but the charge is even more shocking. You cannot read Ezekiel 16 and then think that breaking God's law is some impersonal offense against abstract regulations. Ezekiel 16 makes it very clear that God doesn't see your disobedience that way at all. To the Lord, it is fundamentally personal. His outrage here is not first about law but about relationship.

The word picture depicts a marriage where not only has the bride dishonored her marriage vows, but she has also been soliciting lovers on the street. And not only has she been soliciting lovers on the street, she hasn't asked them to pay her. Rather, in a kind of reverse prostitution, she has paid them to be her lovers. The bride here (the people of Israel) was so anxious to find love anywhere, she went out on the street and paid for it.

It really is true that disobedience is always first about breaking covenantal relationship with God before it is about breaking God's law. Disloyalty to one's relationship with God always leads to disobedience of some kind. But there is more. True love is a state of awe. You are enthralled with the other person, enthralled with what he or she has brought into your life and enthralled that he or she would choose to live with a person like you.

Perhaps you remember, if you are married, the days before your wedding, when you were in a bit of awe that you were going to get married. Perhaps you remember the first few days of your marriage when you would wake up and the awe of being married would hit you again. And perhaps you can relate to that sad, progressive loss of awe and gratitude that often follows. Increasingly you take your spouse for granted. Increasingly you forget the blessing of your relationship. Increasingly you are bored with the repeated cycle of the mundane that settles into every marriage. At this point your eyes and your heart begin to wander. At this point you fantasize about what it would be like to be single or to be with someone else. In the crowd of humanity that you see every day, potential replacement mates catch

your attention, make you wonder, and cause you to hunger for
something other than what you have.

When you come to that place and adultery has captured your
mind and may soon control your body, you don't have a law
problem; you have a marital awe problem. Gratitude and celebration have been replaced by dissatisfaction and complaint.
You are about to step over your marital boundaries because
you've lost your awe.

So it is with every act of disobedience. It is a breaking of a
marital covenant with God that was achieved, signed, sealed,
and paid for by his grace. You've lost your awe, and because
you have, you are capable of doing what you thought you'd
never do. Your heart is capable of wandering because awe of
God no longer holds it captive. You're still shopping for awe
because that quest is hardwired into you, but you're looking for
it horizontally and not vertically. Almost any lover will do at
almost any cost. You're going to break God's laws all over the
place, not because you're looking for laws to break but because
you're an awe amnesiac searching for an awe fix in things that
won't ever satisfy and climbing over God's fences to get what
you think will give that sense of awe back to you again.

How the Ten Commandments Work

And God spoke all these words, saying,

"I am the Lord your God, who brought you out of the
land of Egypt, out of the house of slavery.

"You shall have no other gods before me.

"You shall not make for yourself a carved image, or any
likeness of anything that is in heaven above, or that is in the
earth beneath, or that is in the water under the earth. You
shall not bow down to them or serve them, for I the Lord
your God am a jealous God, visiting the iniquity of the fathers
on the children to the third and the fourth generation of those

who hate me, but showing steadfast love to thousands of those who love me and keep my commandments.

"You shall not take the name of the LORD your God in vain, for the LORD will not hold him guiltless who takes his name in vain.

"Remember the Sabbath day, to keep it holy. Six days you shall labor, and do all your work, but the seventh day is a Sabbath to the LORD your God. On it you shall not do any work, you, or your son, or your daughter, your male servant, or your female servant, or your livestock, or the sojourner who is within your gates. For in six days the LORD made heaven and earth, the sea, and all that is in them, and rested on the seventh day. Therefore the LORD blessed the Sabbath day and made it holy.

"Honor your father and your mother, that your days may be long in the land that the LORD your God is giving you.

"You shall not murder.

"You shall not commit adultery.

"You shall not steal.

"You shall not bear false witness against your neighbor.

"You shall not covet your neighbor's house; you shall not covet your neighbor's wife, or his male servant, or his female servant, or his ox, or his donkey, or anything that is your neighbor's." (Ex. 20:1–17)

There is no escaping the essential order of God's commands. The first four commands have to do with one thing and one thing alone: the worship of God. They represent an uncompromising call to live in a real, committed, day-to-day, heart-gripping, life-shaping awe of God. Why? Because only when awe of God rules my heart will I set everything else in my life in its rightful place. Joyful, perseverant obedience only ever grows in the soil of worship. You see, because worship is not just something I occasionally do but the foundation of who I am and because I worship my way through every moment of every day, if my heart is not given over to the worship of God, it will give itself to the worship of something else. Whatever has captured the awe of my heart will also set the agenda for the things that I desire, think, choose, say, and do. The moral life of every human being is driven and shaped by awe, either awe of God or awe of something in God's creation.

But there is something more to be said. The fourth commandment is particularly interesting for our discussion. The command to reserve the Sabbath "to the LORD your God" is itself a gift of grace. Not only are the Ten Commandments rooted in the awe of God, but also built into the commands is a regular, God-ordained recharge of your awe. God knows how quickly we become awe amnesiacs. God knows that life in this fallen world is a day-to-day war of awe. God knows how easily we replace our awe of the Creator with awe of something in his creation. God knows that awe of God constantly wars with awe of self. As the Creator, who hardwired every aspect of our personhood, he knows that our obedience is fueled by worshipful awe. So he commanded one day in every seven to be reserved for rest from our labors and for personal and corporate reflection on him.

You could argue that every element of the gathered worship of God's people is intended to give people their awe back again. We need a moment to refocus on the grandeur of God's glory and grace. We need to see his awesome wisdom and power again. We need to dwell on his patience and faithfulness again. We need to be stunned by the perfection of his holiness and the righteousness of his judgment again. We need to be encouraged by the awesome truth of his constant presence again. We need to be reminded to rest in his amazing sovereignty again. And we need to be blown away by the reality that, by grace, he is all these things for us. He has unleashed his awesome glory on us!

You see, awe doesn't just remind you of who God is; it redefines for you who you are as his creature and his blood-bought child.

Sadly, not a day passes without us becoming transgressors in some way. We willfully step over God's wise and holy boundaries again and again. We know the law. Theologically, we know it is wise and for our good. We don't transgress because we are ignorant. Think with me. If you're angry and you're up in someone's face, so close that he can feel your breath, saying mean things that you shouldn't say, you're not doing that because you're ignorant of the fact that it is wrong. No, you're doing it because at that moment you don't give a rip what is wrong. At that moment, you are lord sovereign in your life, setting your own rules. You want something, and nothing is going to stop you from getting it. You don't have a law problem; you have an awe problem that causes you to have a law problem. God is not in your thoughts at that moment, let alone ruling your heart. This is the real struggle for all of us in the family rooms, kitchens, bedrooms, apartments, malls, offices, and automobiles of everyday life. Between the "already" and the "not yet," our problem is awe amnesia issuing forth in awe replacement.

So we need constant reminders of God's awesome glory. Thankfully, God has embedded those reminders in his creation. The problem is that we so easily become blind. We look but don't see, and because we don't see, we don't worship, and because we don't worship, we fail to obey. So, in beautiful grace, God has carved out a day for us to stop, look, listen, consider, and worship once again. He invites us to remember the awe that brought us to conviction, living faith, gospel hope, and heart and life transformation. He welcomes us to come together into his presence again and again and again because he knows just how fickle our wandering hearts can be. He knows that we will never live as he has ordained if we do not stand in awe of who he is.

Powerless Law

So where does this leave us? It leaves us with no hope, no plea, no help but the grace of the Lord Jesus Christ. If our disobedience was just a law problem, then perhaps the law could rescue us. But since our lawlessness lives at a profoundly deeper heart level—our propensity to live for ourselves, to write our own rules, and to step over God's boundaries—the law will never fix our transgressions. And let me add that human effort will never fix human immorality. Since I am my biggest problem and since the greatest danger to me is me and since I am never able to escape from myself, I have no capacity whatsoever to fix what is broken. I need help. I need a Redeemer.

The apostle Paul says it this way in Romans 8:3: "For God has done what the law, weakened by the flesh, could not do. By sending his own Son in the likeness of sinful flesh and for sin, he condemned sin in the flesh." Both elements are here: the powerlessness of the law and the weakness of the flesh (sinful nature). I am too weak in every way to help myself, and the law does not have the power to rescue me. The law is able to expose my sin and guide me as to how God wants me to live, but it has no power whatsoever to rescue me from my sin.

Once you admit that you don't just have a behavior-oriented moral problem but, more fundamentally, a heart-located awe problem, you will see that you need more than a system of reform; you need a Redeemer. We must not reduce Christianity to a system of theology and rules. Theology and rules will never redeem you. They were never given by God to be an end in themselves. They are a means to an end. Their purpose is to cause you to see the depth of your need and the sufficiency of Christ's work so that you might run to him in the desperation of faith, placing your hope in his grace and having your heart filled with awe of him.

Transgression is an awe problem before it is a law problem, and for that we need a Redeemer. Thankfully, the Redeemer has come, and his work for you is complete. Turn to him, and you will find the grace you need to see the reality of your awe problem and the hope that only comes through Christ.

7

COMPLAINT

I would maintain that thanks are the highest form of thought;
and that gratitude is happiness doubled by wonder.
G. K. CHESTERTON[6]

I'm about to hurt your feelings. If right now you're complaining about something, you're not complaining because you have a

lack of resources problem,
location problem,
situation problem,
people problem,
suffering problem,
fairness problem,
physical health problem,
church problem,
marriage problem,
employment problem,
parent problem,
life-difficulty problem,
neighbor problem, or
fallen-world problem.

Sure, you may be dealing with difficulty in one or more of these areas, but they are not the cause of your grumbling. Your tendency to complain is rooted at a deeper level. Here's the bottom line: we complain not because we have a stuff-of-life problem but because we have an awe problem. Our problem is not just what we are dealing with but, more foundationally, how our view of God shapes how we see and deal with it. We tend to think of complaining as a little thing, but maybe it's bigger than we realize. Let me use a well-known biblical story to illustrate.

River of Complaint

Read the account that follows carefully:

> Then we set out from Horeb and went through all that great and terrifying wilderness that you saw, on the way to the hill country of the Amorites, as the LORD our God commanded us. And we came to Kadesh-barnea. And I said to you, "You have come to the hill country of the Amorites, which the LORD our God is giving us. See, the LORD your God has set the land before you. Go up, take possession, as the LORD, the God of your fathers, has told you. Do not fear or be dismayed." Then all of you came near me and said, "Let us send men before us, that they may explore the land for us and bring us word again of the way by which we must go up and the cities into which we shall come." The thing seemed good to me, and I took twelve men from you, one man from each tribe. And they turned and went up into the hill country, and came to the Valley of Eshcol and spied it out. And they took in their hands some of the fruit of the land and brought it down to us, and brought us word again and said, "It is a good land that the LORD our God is giving us."
>
> Yet you would not go up, but rebelled against the command of the LORD your God. And you murmured in your tents and said, "Because the LORD hated us he has brought us out of the land of Egypt, to give us into the hand of the Amorites, to destroy us. Where are we going up? Our brothers have made our hearts melt, saying, 'The people are greater

and taller than we. The cities are great and fortified up to heaven. And besides, we have seen the sons of the Anakim there.'" Then I said to you, "Do not be in dread or afraid of them. The LORD your God who goes before you will himself fight for you, just as he did for you in Egypt before your eyes, and in the wilderness, where you have seen how the LORD your God carried you, as a man carries his son, all the way that you went until you came to this place." Yet in spite of this word you did not believe the LORD your God, who went before you in the way to seek you out a place to pitch your tents, in fire by night and in the cloud by day, to show you by what way you should go.

And the LORD heard your words and was angered, and he swore, "Not one of these men of this evil generation shall see the good land that I swore to give to your fathers, except Caleb the son of Jephunneh. He shall see it, and to him and to his children I will give the land on which he has trodden, because he has wholly followed the LORD!" (Deut. 1:19–36)

So that you fully understand this story and the significance of Israel's complaint, I need to set the scene for you. The people of Israel were the chosen children of the Most High God, the Creator of the universe, the sovereign planner of all things, the One who had redeemed them from Egypt and had sustained them in the wilderness. He had placed his covenant love on them and had promised not only that they would be his people but that he would provide for them a land. As the Lord Almighty and in defense of his people, he would defeat all the nations that stood in the way of Israel taking possession of what was theirs by the will of God.

Now the only thing that separated Israel from actually possessing what God had promised was the Jordan River. That river should have been the doorway to their victory; instead, its banks became the scene of their complaint.

They had sent spies into the land to check it out and collect some of the rich produce that grew there, but they collected something else—a whole lot of fear. They came back reporting that the people who lived in the land were not only taller than the Israelites but also lived in great, fortified cities. At this point, with hearts melting with fear, the people of Israel refused to leave their tents and take what God had given them. Instead they sat in their tents complaining against the Lord: "Because the LORD hated us he has brought us out of the land of Egypt, to give us into the hands of the Amorites, to destroy us" (Deut. 1:27). This statement exposes the problem. Israel didn't have just a big-people problem. They didn't have just a fortified-cities problem. They didn't have just a "we're tired after trekking through the wilderness and don't want to have to fight for the land God promised" problem. No, at the bottom of their grumbling was an awe problem.

Of course, what they were facing was bigger than their natural ability. Of course, they would have to be willing to fight battles. Of course, the possession of the land would be difficult. Life in this fallen world is hard. God does orchestrate difficulties in my life that I would never have chosen to face. But the words of Israel demonstrate that their complaint was not just about their circumstances but about God. If praise is celebrating God's awesome glory, then complaint is antipraise. Not only does complaint fail to recognize his grandeur, it questions his power and character. If you believe that God is the Creator and controller of all that is, then it is impossible to complain about your circumstances without complaining about God. Complaint is awelessness verbalized.

Awelessness that leads me to question God's power and character will cause me to take my life into my own hands, and because I have taken my life into my own hands, I will rebel against what God calls me to do. This is what took place on the banks of the Jordan River. Far from simple grumbling about difficult circumstances, Israel's complaint was deeply theological and morally rebellious. You simply cannot understand this story and walk away thinking that, for the believer, complaining is a little thing. This passage clearly shows that God does not view it as a little thing at all. He was swift in his critique and judgment. Because Israel questioned the Lord, they would not see the land of promise. How tragic! Let's further unpack the awe problem in this narrative.

Five Questions That Steal or Seal Your Hope

It is quite clear that your view of God will inescapably shape your perspective on your circumstances. In this way your theology is like a lens through which you examine life. This means you never come at your circumstances from some happy place of neutrality. You and I are always evaluating our situation from the vantage point of vertical awe or awelessness. In some way, we, like the children of Israel, are always asking and answering five deeply theological questions, and the way that we answer them will push us toward hope or panic.

And it is important to say that you answer these questions in some way every day. Every day you and I theologize about our lives. In this way, our functional, street-level theology may fundamentally influence our daily living more than our formal theology. The unconscious theology that we embrace may differ significantly from the theology that we say we believe when we are making conscious theological commitments. The God in our formal outlines may be very different from the God we think about every day in those moments when we are unaware that we are thinking about him. You ask and answer these profoundly significant theological questions every day whether you are a pastor, a computer programmer, an office assistant, a student, or a plumber. And you do so in a state of either vertical awe or awe amnesia.

1. Is God good? Now you can rest assured that the goodness of God will confuse you. You see, what looks good from God's perfect eternity-to-destiny perspective doesn't always seem good to us at ground level. It is hard to accept that God knows better than we do. It is hard to admit that God can use difficulties for good in our lives. When it comes to what is good, it is very hard for us to stay on God's agenda. And again the issue of awe lies at the heart of this. If I live at the center of my God-given capacity for awe—that is, if awe of self has replaced awe of God—then I will invariably conclude that God is not always good, and loads of complaints will follow.

If I am at the center, I will define *good* as what is comfortable, predictable, pleasurable, natural, and easy. The good life will be the easy life because awe of self will have replaced awe of God as the principal motivator of my life. So when difficulty comes my way, my default theological response will be to wonder why God is doing what he is doing and to question his goodness. In my early days of ministry, I was blown away by how many of the people whom I counseled were angry with God. I was amazed at how many people no longer assumed that God was good.

Now here's what's deadly about this. As I have mentioned earlier in this book and elsewhere, if you allow yourself to question God's goodness, you will quit following his commands, and you will quit running to him for help because you will no longer rely on, follow, or seek the help of someone you no longer trust. But God *is* good. His goodness is the foundation stone of his awesome qualities. He never thinks, desires, says, or does what is evil. He is the definition of all that is good, right, and true. Everything he does is good in every way. His goodness is so bright and glorious it should leave us breathless, silent, and amazed. And if we are amazed at his goodness, we won't panic in times of trouble, and we won't refuse to do the hard things he calls us to do.

I wish I could say that I've never brought God into the court of my judgment or questioned his goodness, but I have. For three years I housed my aging father, whose sin had devastated our family. I hoped I would be an agent of his confession and repentance, but it never happened. One day he fell on the steps in my house, slipped into a coma, and died. In my view, there was nothing good about the whole story. Housing him seemed to have been a colossal waste. In a hospital elevator, all the pent-up anger came gushing out of me. I was glad that I was alone. The way I angrily questioned God's goodness scared me. It was humbling that for even one moment I would allow myself to think that I knew better than God, that my "good" was better than the good he had willed for me. What about you? Does awe of God's goodness interpret life for you? Or do the hardships of life cause you to question his goodness?

2. *Will God do what he promised?* Few questions in life are more important than this one. Since we are all small and weak, since we never really know what is going to happen next, and since God calls us to do difficult, sacrificial things, we need to know that his promises are reliable. Will he be with us always? Will he give us everything we need? Will he forgive us no matter what? Will his love last forever? Will he stay with the work of his grace until that work is done? Will he provide the guidance and protection that we need? Will he?

God's promises are meant to move and motivate us. They are meant to instill hope. They are meant to give us courage. They are meant to defeat feelings of loneliness, inability, and fear. They are meant to give us peace when things around us are chaotic and confusing. God's promises are meant to blow your mind and settle your heart. They are his gifts of grace to you. In your heart of hearts, you know you could never have earned the riches that he pours down on you. His promises are meant to leave you in awe of him and in wonder at the glory of his grace. His promises are designed to be the way that you interpret and make sense of your life.

I am amazed at the numbers of believers I meet who are in some state of spiritual paralysis because they no longer believe the promises of God. Because they don't believe the promises of God, they don't have much reason to continue doing the radical things that God calls every one of his children to do. When doubt replaces awe, you will soon give up on all the gospel disciplines of the Christian life. Your problem isn't that life is hard. Your problem is that you've lost your awe of the God who made the promises that once motivated the way you dealt with life. Do you stand with hope and courage on the awesome promises of God? Or do you walk through the quicksand of questioning their reliability?

3. Is God in control? Here is a fundamentally important place for your awe to rest. In some ways, all the other questions rest on this one. It would make no good difference in life if God didn't rule the places that resist his goodness. God's promises are only as trustworthy as the extent of his control. He can only guarantee that he will do something in the places where he has absolute control. What good is his almighty power if he lacks the authority to exercise it? It is of no comfort to know that God is in control if he does not rule over the circumstances where his care is essential. Yes, all the comfort of God's awesome qualities rests on his sovereign control over every situation, location, and person.

But here's the problem: at ground level, your world doesn't

look to be under careful and wise control. In fact, at times it seems totally out of control. This gets us right back to the same place we have been with each of these questions. Will you let your interpretation of circumstances tell you who God is, or will you allow God's awesome revelation of himself to interpret your circumstances for you? You see, people who live in fear, who beat themselves up with way too many "what if" questions, or who have trouble turning off their minds when they go to bed don't have a circumstances problem; they have an awe problem. You and I will only rest in situations over which we have no control if we are in awe of the One who controls them all for his glory and for our good.

People who have to be in control don't first have a power problem; they have an awe problem, which produces power hunger. A lack of awe at the sovereignty of God causes them to try to establish personal peace and safety by means of personal control. What about you? Has your awe of God's infinite sovereignty freed you from both fear and the need to be in control?

4. *Does God have the needed power?* How do you measure the power of God? How can poor, feeble minds grasp that which is without limit? Scripture tells us that God comes to us with the same power by which he raised Christ from the dead. Now that's a definition of ultimate power! What in the universe would be more powerful than the ability to speak life into a dead body? What could be a better definition of almighty power than to be able to rise up and walk away from being dead? There is no place where human beings are more powerless than in death.

If you've experienced the death of a loved one, you know what it is like. I stood next to my mom's bed after she had died and wished for one more conversation, wished I could hear her say "I love you" one more time, wished that she could squeeze my hand and say it would be okay. I wished with all that was in me for more, but she was gone, and I was powerless to do anything about it.

God's power is so great that he rules life and death. Now here's why this matters. You will only have peace in the face of your own weaknesses, failures, foibles, and inabilities when you are in awe of God's awesome power. You will only rise up to do what you don't have the natural ability to do when you know that God's awesome power is with you. Awe of God's power produces courage in the face of weakness. Awe of God's power enables you to admit your limits and yet live with courage and hope. Timidity, fear, denial, hiding, excusing, and running away are not first weakness problems but awe problems. I step into what is bigger than me because I know the One who is with me is bigger than what I am facing. What about you? How much of what you do is done out of fear and not faith? How often are you paralyzed by your weakness? Does awe of God's power cause you to live a forward-moving and courageous life?

5. Does God care about me? Perhaps this is the question we're most conscious of. It's the question that the bullied teenager asks. It's the question asked by the wife who has watched her marriage go sour. It's the question the exhausted parent asks at the end of a very hard day with children. It's the question asked by the lonely single woman. The man who has just lost his job asks this question. It's what's asked by the person who with sadness has left the church that has lost its way. It's what the person suffering the weaknesses of old age asks. It's what the person asks who is struggling through a long illness. It's what you wonder about as you watch the surrounding culture coarsen and worsen.

God's care *is* foundational. It lets me know that all that he is, he is for me. His care means he will be good *for me*. His care means he will do what he promised *for me*. His care means he will exercise his control *for me*. His care means he will unleash his awesome power *for me*. Awe of his care allows me to embrace the hope found in all of his other qualities. The Bible never debates God's care; it assumes and declares it. It confronts you with the lavish nature of his mercy, love, patience, forbearance, grace, tenderness, and faithfulness. He is the ultimate loving Father. He is the completely faithful Friend. He is the One who stays closer than a brother. He alone will never leave you, no matter what. He is the One who never sends you without going with you. He is your protector, guide, defender, teacher, Savior, and healer. He never mocks your weakness but gives you strength. He never uses your sin against you but affords you forgiveness. He never plays favorites, never wants to give up on you, never gets exhausted or wishes he could quit. He never plays with you. He is never disloyal. His care is so awesome and so complete that nothing in your life's experience in any way compares. He cares!

What about you? Do you go through times of disappointment and complaining because you have allowed yourself to question his care? The size of your hope is directly related to the level of your awe of God's care.

So every word spoken in complaint, every murmur of grumbling is deeply theological. Our problem is not that the "good life" has passed us by, that people have failed us, or that life has been hard. All these things have happened to us because we live in a broken world. And if our contentment rests on life being easy, comfortable, and pleasurable, we'll have no contentment this side of eternity. We complain so much not because we have horizontal problems but because we have a vertical problem. Only when the awe of God rules your heart will you be able to have joy even when people disappoint you and life gets hard. Awe means your heart will be filled more with a sense of blessing than with a sense of want. You will be daily blown away by what you have been given rather than being constantly disturbed by what you think you need. Awe produces gratitude, gratitude instills joy, and the harvest of joy is contentment.

Tomorrow there is a good possibility that complaint will be on your lips, and when it is, cry out for your Savior's help. He alone can open your eyes to his glory. His grace alone can satisfy your heart. And as you cry out, remember that he is so rich in grace that he will never turn a deaf ear to your cries.

MATERIALISM

Vision is the art of seeing things invisible.
JONATHAN SWIFT[7]

The designer sneakers
The hot sports car
The top-tier filet mignon
The exotic vacation
The $75,000 remodeled kitchen
The huge suburban home
The expensive watch
The gorgeous dress
The new nose
The toned body
The next tattoo
The carefully collected antiques
The well-manicured lawn
The sixty-inch flat screen
The lavish wedding
The beautiful garden
The seldom-used set of fine china

What do the things on this list have in common, and what in the world do they have to do with the topic of this book? Above is a seemingly random list of material things. None of them is inherently evil, but together they may depict a massive problem many of us have with the material world. I am not about to suggest that you jettison all the beautiful material things in your life. I am not about to suggest that it is evil to possess or enjoy these things. But I will suggest that street-level materialism is capturing our hearts and eating up the time, energy, and resources of our lives. For many of us, something is fundamentally amiss in our relationship to the world of physical things with which we come in contact every day.

I am deeply persuaded that the problem lies not with the things that attract us, addict us, and eat up our lives. Rather, our problem is what we bring to those things, which renders us unable to control our desire for, and our seemingly endless acquisition and enjoyment of, them.

The Search for Life

Why do we keep acquiring more possessions when we clearly already have enough?

Why do we so often envy what other people have?

Why do we eat more than we need to eat to be healthy?

Why do we tend to live in a house way larger than our family truly needs?

Why are we so obsessed about our physical appearance and fitness?

Why do we employ modern medical technologies to ward off old age?

Why are so many of us in debt?

Why do we stare into overstuffed closets and tell ourselves that we have nothing to wear?

Why do we eat out so often?

Why do we invest so much time and money in our vacations?

Why does illicit sex seduce so many of us?

Why? I am deeply persuaded that materialism is not first a "thing" problem but an awe problem. We cannot control our lust for things because our capacity for awe has been kidnapped. We find it nearly impossible to be content because the vertical awe that produces contentment is not functioning in our hearts the way God intended it to. Only when awe of God is in its rightful place in our hearts will the physical things around us be in their appropriate places in our lives.

Let's examine the underlying spiritual dynamics of our struggle with material things.

1. Everyone is searching for life. It's hardwired inside all of us. Because God created us as spiritual beings to have a relationship with him, we are all on a bit of a frantic, personal, story-shaping quest for life. We are hunting for contentment, satisfaction, joy, hope, courage, meaning and purpose, a reason to get up in the morning, peace of heart, confidence that we are on the right path and doing the right thing, fulfillment, security, an internal sense of well-being, freedom from fear and dread, and identity. We are searching for life, and there are only two places to look. You can look to the Creator for life or you can search for life in what he created. But there is one thing for sure: you will search for life.

2. You will be in awe of what you think will give you life. Your search for life is at the center of your world of awe. You and I will tend to be captivated by, controlled by, and in awe of whatever we think will give us awe. The future bride is in awe of her fiancé because she thinks he offers her life, life as she has never known it before. The new hire is in awe of his new job because he thinks his job will be a major component in the "good life" he has always hungered for. The couple is vibrating with excitement as they turn the key to their new house because they think they will find and make life there. The athlete can't believe he has just signed his first professional contract; it's all he ever wanted out of life. The wealthy businessman has gained lots of weight over the past several years pursuing and enjoying too much success. The Hare Krishna convert is so excited because he thinks he has finally found the key to life. The old man is depressed and bitter because he feels that life has passed him by. The teenager will cross any boundaries you try to set for him in his anxious and immature search for life. The divorced woman can't deal with the fact that the unfaithfulness of another person has taken life from her. The couple loads another several thousand dollars on their credit card in yet another attempt to buy life. Thousands of us look over the fence every day at someone else and envy their existence because we think that they've found life. No matter who you are, no matter where you are, and no matter your gender or age, you either tell yourself that you have life or you are on a quest to find life, and you will tend to be in awe of whatever you think will give you life. God made us to search for life.

3. *Material things are a miserable place to look for life.* The mistake we all make is the moment-by-moment, day-to-day loss of our awe. This tragic mistake is the overarching theme of every word in this book. It is why we tend to be so spiritually empty, so consistently unfulfilled, and so driven to fill up our lives with so many things. It is why we tend to be anxious and depressed. It is why we tend to be more jealous than thankful. It is why so many of us are unhappy. It is why we all tend to be looking for the next big thing. We make the profound mistake of looking horizontally for what can only be found vertically. Material things capture our awe and, in so doing, dominate our lives because we mistakenly think they can give us the one thing that they will never give—life. I find myself saying to people, "Earth will never be your savior." We know it theologically, but

it seems to get lost in the pursuits of everyday life. And because it does, we repeat to ourselves, "If only I had _____, then my life would be _____."

So let's consider God's purpose for material things.

1. Material things are for your sustenance. You and I literally could not live without the material world that surrounds us. The flora and fauna around us provide nutrition and health for us. The liquid in our world keeps us hydrated. We could not live if there was no physical air to breathe. Material things provide shelter and warmth for us. Material things protect and transport us. Material things give covering to our bodies and shade to our eyes. Material things defend us against disease and help cure the diseases that have inflicted us.

The proper relationship to the physical world is not to hate it, to separate yourself from it as much as possible. No, you should celebrate how God in his infinite wisdom and love built a physical world that sustains you. You and I should be amazed at the grace that is exhibited by the fact that the world God made sustains us even in those moments when we ignore him, are angry with him, or rebel against his will for us. It should astonish us that we don't have to earn the right to have the earth sustain us. This is God's good gift to us all. The physical realm is not just designed to give God glory but is also carefully designed to provide for us what we physically need.

2. Material things are for your pleasure. Biblical faith doesn't curse the material world, and it is not antipleasure. God created a gloriously beautiful and pleasurable world. Consider the multihued vista of a sunset. Think about the gorgeous coat of a zebra. Listen to the melodious songs of the birds. Consider the vast array of colors, textures, and tastes of the food you eat. Imagine standing in front of a masterpiece painting or listening to a famous piece of music. Think of the beauty of the grain of wood or the swirling stripes that course their way through a piece of marble. Remember the pleasure of a kiss or the succulence of a ripe piece of fruit.

God designed his world to give you pleasure every day in a variety of ways. And God carefully built pleasure gates into your physical and emotional being. Your eyes, ears, nose, mouth, hands, mind, and emotions all enable you to take in and enjoy the pleasures that God has embedded into the physical world that surrounds you. For instance, God did not decide that you would be physically fed by a tasteless gray pill. He unleashed his creativity on your diet so that you can consume an almost endless variety of smells, tastes, colors, and textures. So eating is not just a habit of sustenance, it is one of life's greatest pleasures.

You should never feel guilty for pursuing, participating in, and enjoying the pleasures of the material world God created. What you and I need to guard against is allowing awe of those pleasures to become the principal motivator of our hearts. When awe of material things rules your heart, then you will live for material things, and when you live for material things, you will do just about anything to gain them, maintain them, keep them, and enjoy them. This is precisely what Jesus is addressing in Matthew 6:19–33. (It would be helpful if you would stop now and read this passage). Such a materialistic attitude is not only morally dangerous but is also a violation of the reason for which you and I were created. It is wrong for material cravings to dominate our hearts and lifestyles.

But this is what sin does to all of us. It causes us to exchange awe of the Creator for awe of the created thing. We try to fill our spiritual hunger with the material world. We end up defining ourselves and the good of our lives by the size of our pile of physical stuff. We say we love God, but our lives become controlled and directed by the frenetic pursuit of material satisfaction. We live with worry about what we have and envious anxiety about what we don't have. We possess much, but we always feel needy. We own much, but we're always acquiring. We tend to find much more pleasure in receiving than in giving. In our individual economic worlds, no matter how much we make, income always seems to chase lifestyle. We live in debt, but we don't stop spending. We own so much that we have no more space, so we rent storage units for more stuff. We get fat and addicted and fall into debt, but that does not stop us. Our obsession with material things brings trouble and heartache into our lives. So we tell ourselves that we'll do better—we commit ourselves for a time to new budgets, we go on temporary diets, we hold garage sales. But none of it lasts for long because deep inside us, we treasure the creation more than we treasure the Creator.

Material pleasure is one of spirituality's most significant battlefronts between the "already" of our conversion and the "not yet" of our home going. This deep spiritual war rages in our lives every day. And it rages not because we have a pleasure problem but because we have an awe problem that produces a pleasure problem. When awe of the creation replaces awe of the Creator in your life, you will have a very difficult time controlling your desire for and pursuit of material things. Our material addiction is rooted in awe replacement. Only when awe of God rules your heart will you be able to keep the pleasures of the material world in their proper place.

I can't leave this discussion without again saying that God provides grace for this struggle. God's grace aims for the rescue, transformation, and deliverance of your heart. God's grace works to free you from bondage to your own desires. God's grace battles for your thoughts and desires even when you don't. God's grace is powerful and unrelenting. You and I have no ability whatsoever to liberate ourselves from ourselves, but

God's grace does. And this grace—our only hope—is not something you earn by your prayers of guilt or by your material asceticism; you and I can never earn this grace by anything we do. It is God's eternal gift to us. We will only find hope for our battle with material things in the forgiving, liberating, and transforming power of this grace. And this grace will fight for us until it finally wins the war of awe so that material things will never again lay claim to our hearts. Even so, Lord Jesus, come quickly!

3. *Material things are for your remembrance.* All the variegated glory of the material world has a purpose in God's plan. The One who made us owns us and loves us. He knows how quickly we forget. He knows how quickly awe of him is replaced by awe of what he made. He knows that we all tend to be recovering from or heading toward our next moment of vertical awe amnesia. So in tender love and grace, he purposefully designed the material world to point to him. He doesn't hide his existence, character, and glory from us, keeping it only for the superspiritual elite. No, everyone who has eyes to see, ears to hear, and a heart to receive encounters him every day in and through what he made (see Psalm 19 and Romans 1). The physical world itself is meant to be one big constant reminder of the One of infinite power and glory who fashioned every part of it and holds it together by the power of his will.

Now this means you should have two types of awe in your life. First, you should exercise *remembrance awe*. This is the kind of awe you are to have for the created world. The physical world is amazing. It should leave you in awe but in a specific type of awe. It should produce in you the awe of remembrance. Every beautiful vista, every intriguing sound, every amazing thing should remind you of the God of glory who created and stands behind it all. It's wrong not to be in awe of what God created, but it's even more deeply wrong when you can look at created glory without remembering God.

Here's the point: *remembrance awe* should immediately stimulate in us the second and deeper awe, *worship awe*. The glories of the created world are intended to cause you to worship the God of glory who made and controls them. Remembrance awe is meant to awaken and stimulate your heart. Worship awe is meant to capture your heart and bend your knee in humble, joyful adoration. We all get into spiritual difficulty when remembrance awe becomes worship awe, when we begin to worship the creation and forget the Creator. As I stated earlier, this is the battle of battles, that the thing created to stimulate worship in you becomes instead the object of your worship. In little mundane moments, we do this again and again. Craving for the next physical thing that we think we need becomes more important to us than God's existence, character, plan, and grace.

I say it jokingly, but I am serious at the same time: there are days when I don't care about redemption; all I want is a good steak. There are days when I don't care about God; I just want nice weather for a change. There are times when I don't care about God's will; I just want the people in my life to like me. There are moments when I don't think about the beauty of God's grace; I just want a little control over my schedule. It's sad, but I must confess that I sometimes stop at remembrance awe and don't allow it to stimulate worship awe in my heart, and because I do, I still need the grace that alone has the power to rescue me from me.

4. Material things can never give you life. You and I need to remember that the physical world around us was never designed to give us life. It can give us temporary fulfillment. It can give us a short-term emotional buzz. It can give us beauty that provides momentary distraction and retreat. It can entertain and educate us, but it cannot offer the one thing every human being desperately craves: life. This whole discussion begs the question asked in Isaiah 55. The first nine verses of this passage contain one of the most beautiful word pictures of God's free gift of grace in the entire Bible. It's a passage that you and I should return to again and again because we need this picturesque language to reorient our minds to the gospel. In the middle of the amazing glories of the created world, you can lose your mind and become obsessed with cravings, thinking that you're desperately needy when, in fact, you are both well loved and lavishly supplied.

The question in this passage is *the* question. It really does capture the everyday battle that we all have with the material world. Here it is: "Why do you spend your money for that which is not bread, and your labor for that which does not satisfy?" (v. 2). In words that paint pictures in your mind, the prophet essentially says that God is the only food that will ever satisfy your heart. Eating anything else will leave you hungry and dissatisfied. But that's what we all do at some point. We tell ourselves that if we only had _____, then we would be happy and content. But we never are because our souls will never be satisfied until they find their satisfaction in him.

Could it be that you struggle with material things because you've stayed at *remembrance awe* and stopped that from leading you into *worship awe*? Is there evidence in your life that you are looking for life where it will never be found? Here's the bottom line: when awe of the creation replaces awe of the Creator, you will have a terrible time controlling your craving for and pursuit of material things. Biblical literacy and theological knowledge won't help you, because, at the deepest level of the motivation of your heart, a deadly exchange has taken place, and because it has, you keep running after the created world, hoping that it will be your personal messiah. So you look to your possessions or your marriage or your job or the next location or the next experience to give you life, but it never does—you always come up empty. And Isaiah would ask, "Why do you labor so hard for what does not satisfy?"

Grace to Beat Guilt

Now all this could be very discouraging to consider if you were left to the limited resources of your own wisdom and strength, but as God's child, you're not. The Creator of the physical world is also your "I am with you always" Savior. He not only offers you resources, he gives you himself. He makes you the place where he dwells, in powerful protecting, rescuing, transforming, and delivering grace. He meets you with strength in moments when you are weak. He graces you with wisdom in moments when you're acting as a fool. He fights for your soul even when you don't fight for yourself. He doesn't wait for you to measure up. No, he measures up for you in every situation and in every way so that, when you don't measure up, you receive mercy and not judgment.

So you don't have to hide your materialism in shame. You don't have to hide the guilt of your material craving. You don't have to work to explain away your debt. You can run into God's presence in weakness and failure knowing full well that you will receive his love and his restorative grace. Admit it. You're like me. At times your awe of the material world replaces your awe of the God who made the material. But as you admit this, don't run from God. Run to him, and find mercy and grace that form-fits to your particular need and your unique struggle.

9

GROWTH

You will never cease to be the most amazed person on earth at what God has done for you on the inside.
OSWALD CHAMBERS[8]

If someone asked you what the two most important questions you could ask were, what would you answer? If you are God's child, there may be no more important questions than these two:

What in the world is God doing right here, right now?

And how in the world should I respond to it?

How would you answer these questions, and how would your answer shape the way you think about God, yourself, life, what is important, and what you should daily give yourself to?

Because Sharon didn't answer these questions well, she was perennially depressed. Since Joe didn't answer these questions well, he spent much of his life angry. Since Joslynn didn't answer these questions well, her heart was constantly eaten by envy. Because Frank didn't answer these questions well, he was all too driven by material success. Since Judy didn't answer these questions well, she was entirely too focused on what others thought of her. Brad never answered these questions well, and as an old man, he looked back on his life with bitterness and regret.

Sharon, Joe, Joslynn, Frank, Judy, and Brad were all believers, but they all lived dissatisfied lives, thinking that somehow the good life had passed them by. They were all confused by God's promises. They all wondered why he hadn't come through for them, and each of their stories was a narrative of an ever-weakening faith. They never really understood God's agenda between the "already" and the "not yet," and because they didn't, their faith didn't rescue, encourage, protect, comfort, or guide them. Their faith was relegated to the "spiritual/religious" part of their lives but never became the overarching lifestyle that gave sense and meaning to all they did.

I think thousands of people remain in the same place as my friends. God confuses them, Christianity confuses them, living by faith confuses them, grace confuses them, and so their walk with God is very different from what they imagined it would be. Between the "already" of their new birth and the "not yet" of their final home going, they were gloriously forgiven and lavishly loved by God, but sadly, they lived like lost souls. They simply never understood or got on God's agenda. Their Christianity lived most vibrantly on Sunday, but it was more a formal religious habit than a radical new way of living. None of them talked much about their faith to others because they just didn't have much spiritual enthusiasm to share. I often wonder how many truly forgiven people live like lost souls, wandering through their Christian life like someone in a strange city with no map or GPS. I wonder how many truly forgiven people are lost in their job, lost in their marriage, lost in parenting, lost in their pile of possessions, lost in their pursuit of success—forgiven, but lost in the journey between the "already" and the "not yet."

What is God doing right now? Well, if justification is an

event that secures our forgiveness and acceptance with God, then sanctification is a process that works the radical transformation of our hearts. This lifelong process of radical personal heart and life transformation is the Redeemer's focused zeal between the "already" and the "not yet." Justification is God's totally complete work to purchase your forgiveness. Sanctification is God's ongoing work to change and grow you.

You see, God hasn't promised you a good job or great kids. He hasn't promised you an easy marriage and a comfortable place to live. He hasn't promised you physical health and a good church to attend. He hasn't promised that you would experience affluence and be surrounded by things that entertain you. What he has promised is that he will complete the work that he has begun in you. And if you're honest, you will admit that you exhibit empirical evidence every day that you still need to change. Maybe that's seen in a moment of irritation, pride, impatience, envy, lust, greed, or doubt. Maybe it's seen in an act of rebellion, vengeance, or harsh and unkind words. Maybe it's seen in cheating a little on your taxes, slightly bending the truth as you tell a story, or going to a website that you shouldn't visit. Maybe it's seen in subtle racism or in hoarding blessings that you should share. Maybe it's anger in traffic or impatience in the line at the convenience store. But it's there and you know it, evidence that you are not yet all that God in his grace can make you. You and I may be satisfied with who we are, but God isn't satisfied and will not quit until his work is done.

At this point you may be thinking, "Paul, this all makes sense, but I'm confused as to what it has to do with a book on the awe of God." Permit me to explain.

What Sin Does to All of Us

You'll never understand what God is doing right here, right now until you understand what sin does to the way that your heart functions. We all know that sin makes all of us *lawbreakers*, but many of us miss the fact that sin does something much more foundationally destructive in our hearts. Sin makes all of us *awe breakers*.

A verse in 2 Corinthians 5 explains this concept of being an awe breaker. It says that Jesus lived and died so that "those who live might no longer live for themselves" (v. 15). Here's what this powerful little phrase means: people whose every thought, desire, word, and action was meant to be motivated and shaped by awe of God, exchange awe of God for awe of self. It's not just that sin makes us rebels and fools. It's not just that sin makes us want to write our own laws. No, sin does something more fundamental to each of us. Sin captures and redirects the motivational system of our hearts. In a practically life-shaping way, sin changes how our hearts operate. Paul is talking here about two opposite perspectives on life. In one, the heart is filled with a vision of what I want for me and my little world; in the other, the heart is filled with wonder at who Christ is and what he has done. Each is driven by awe, either awe of personal glory or awe of the glory of Christ. Though we were created to be moved by the awe of God, sin causes our hearts to be moved by the small, individualistic agenda of awe of self. Because we break God's awe design, we then proceed to break God's law design. Let me say it as clearly and practically as I can. Because of sin, *awe of God is very quickly replaced by awe of self.*

What this means is that we don't think, desire, purpose, want, or plan as we should. We want our will to be done. We want the freedom to do what we want to do when we want to do it. We want our lives to be comfortable and our days predictable. We want the people around us to appreciate, indulge, and serve us. We don't want people to disagree with us or tell us that we are wrong. We want affluence without hard work, and we want to do what pleases us without consequences. Sin leaves us tragically broken at the deepest of motivational levels, that is, at the level of our capacity for awe.

Now when God draws you to himself, you are completely forgiven and unconditionally accepted by him, but the battle for the awe of your heart continues. Yes, your heart is now awake to God's glory in a way it has never been, but you still have awe conflict inside. There are still huge motivational battles to be won. This war for awe is really what the lifelong process of change for the Christian—sanctification—is all about. It's not just about learning the correct theology and the right rules. If all we needed were theology and rules, the earth-invading person and work of Jesus simply wouldn't have been necessary. Sanctification is really about the grace of God doing for us what we can't do for ourselves: recapture our awe for God and God alone.

Spiritual growth is about recapturing your awe. The more that the awe of God rules the motivation systems of your heart, the more you will love his kingdom and find pleasure in his work and satisfaction in doing his will. Romans 12:2 talks of being "transformed by the renewal of your mind." There it is. The mind is where change needs to take place. If grace does not transform my motivation, it will not alter my living.

God Battles for Your Awe

Since you are unable to run from or change your heart, you must depend on God's powerful, transforming grace to do for you what you cannot do for yourself. God knew that, and that's why he didn't just forgive you. That forgiveness is a wonderful thing, but he did something else so amazing and mysterious that it is almost impossible to get it inside our finite little brains: he sent his Spirit to live inside you. His Spirit does battle with your flesh. Since this battle rages deep within the motivational system of your heart, it must be fought from the inside out. Knowledge is wonderful but not enough. Rules are incredibly helpful, but they lack the power to do what needs to be done. Sin has kidnapped your awe and put you in the center of your awe, where God alone should be.

Paul tells the Corinthian Christians to "be reconciled to God" (2 Cor. 5:20). Now what does that mean? If they're believers, aren't they already reconciled to God? Well, in this passage, Paul uses the term *reconciliation* in two ways. First is the positional reconciliation of justification. On the basis of Christ's work, I have been reconciled to God, that is, accepted into his presence and adopted into his family. But Paul uses *reconciliation* in another way: the reconciliation of sanctification. Here it is: to the degree that my capacity for awe is ruled or controlled by something or someone other than God, to that degree I need to be further reconciled to God. That's the war of sanctification. It is a war of reconciliation. It is a war to reclaim my awe for God and God alone.

Thankfully, you and I don't fight that war alone. Look at what Paul says to the Galatian believers: "But I say, walk by the Spirit, and you will not gratify the desires of the flesh. For the desires of the flesh are against the Spirit, and the desires of the Spirit are against the flesh, for these are opposed to each other, to keep you from doing the things you want to do" (Gal. 5:16–17). You see, spiritual growth is about the recapture of your thoughts, desires, and motivations, which depends on the recapture of your awe. The goal is that you and I would no longer live for ourselves but live joyfully and willingly for God. We pursue and participate in the work of the Spirit as he works inside us to liberate us from our bondage to ourselves.

The Recapture of Your Awe at
Street Level: A Portrait

Galatians 5 actually presents two awe portraits. Each gives a picture of how what controls your awe controls your living. The first portrait depicts the lifestyle of an awe breaker. Remember that sin causes all of us to become awe thieves. We take the awe that was meant to cause us to worship God and direct it toward ourselves. We put ourselves where God alone was meant to be, making our lives all about us. Now that doesn't mean that when you're living for yourself, you will do all the things described in Galatians 5, but these are the kinds of things that result when awe of God is replaced by awe of self.

Portrait #1: "Now the works of the flesh are evident: sexual immorality, impurity, sensuality, idolatry, sorcery, enmity, strife, jealousy, fits of anger, rivalries, dissensions, divisions, envy, drunkenness, orgies, and things like these. I warn you, as I warned you before, that those who do such things will not inherit the kingdom of God" (Gal. 5:19–21). This list is very helpful and instructive. Notice what unifies all these sin words: self. These are the kinds of things you fall into when, at the deepest level of the motivational system of your heart, you are living for you.

For example, when awe of self has replaced awe of God (i.e., when you are living for you), you will find it very hard to say no to you. You will find it very hard to stay inside the moral boundaries that someone else has set for you. So it will be difficult for you to harness your desire for personal pleasure, and you'll be a sitting duck for sexual immorality and impurity. Your living will be morally shaped more by your physical senses and pleasure than by moral commitments. Because personal pleasure will mean too much to you, you will ask it to do for you what it cannot do, going back again and again for more and soon finding yourself addicted to what you thought you could control (drunkenness). Because you are living for you, you will find it hard to deal with the reality that others have what you don't (jealousy, envy). And because awe of self has replaced awe of God, you will be mad at anything or anyone who happens to get in the way of what you want. You'll be better at making war than peace (enmity, fits of anger, rivalries, strife, dissensions).

You see, all the dark, sad brokenness in the human community that results in such hurt, pain, disillusionment, and disappointment is rooted in a deeper brokenness. Sin is profoundly larger than simply doing the wrong things. Behavioral sin grows out of the malfunctioning, corrupted motivational system of the heart. You simply cannot live for yourself and stay inside God's boundaries. You cannot live in a greater awe of you than of God and live the way God designed you to live.

Here's the point of this portrait: because we are all sinners, this kind of living is intuitive and natural for us. Have you ever lived a conflict-free week? Do you ever get jealous of someone or envious of another's blessing? Have you ever struggled to harness your desire for the pleasures of sex, food, or drink? Have you ever brought strife into your life because you said or did something that was unloving or unkind? If we were honest, we would have to say that this list describes every single one of us. It is a shockingly accurate portrait of the life of every sinner. Why? Because sin makes all of us awe breakers. We all put ourselves in God's place. We all enthrone ourselves in the center of our worlds. All sinners forget God and crown themselves, and what follows is massive moral and interpersonal dysfunction. This is not a here's-how-the-bad-guys-live list. No, this is a what-sin-does-to-all-of-us list.

Portrait #2: "But the fruit of the Spirit is love, joy, peace, patience, kindness, goodness, faithfulness, gentleness, self-control; against such things there is no law. And those who belong to Christ Jesus have crucified the flesh with its passions and desires" (Gal. 5:22–24). Now what holds all these beautiful character qualities together? They all result from living for something bigger than you. This portrait shows how a person's street-level living is transformed when the motivational system of his or her heart begins to be ruled by awe of God rather than awe of self. The agenda that drives every one of these things is bigger than personal pleasure and control.

Let me comment on what this list represents. These character qualities are not moral goals for you to achieve. You and I have no independent ability to produce these things in ourselves because we have no capacity for changing the motivational direction of our hearts. Even though God, in amazing grace, has forgiven us, too many of the things in the previous list still plague our lives. We still desperately need to grow. The clue to the nature of this character list lies in its identification as the "fruit of the Spirit." These things are just not natural for us. They only ever result from the powerful transforming presence of the Spirit of God in our hearts. He comes to reside within our hearts to do in and for us the one thing we can't do for ourselves: reclaim the motivational system of our hearts for God and God alone. The gospel is that Jesus not only died for your forgiveness but also died for your growth and transformation. Jesus died so that between the "already" and the "not yet," we would progressively become people that this portrait displays. And you and I need grace for this transformation as much as we needed grace for our initial acceptance with God.

Look at the list and consider with me how reclaiming awe leads to transformed lives. What keeps us from loving others? Isn't it always love of self that gets in the way of a consistent and practical love for others? Here's the point: only people who keep the first great commandment will ever keep the second great commandment. Only when God is in his rightful place will others be in the appropriate place in my heart and life. Only when I love God above all else will I ever love others as myself. How about joy? The DNA of joy is gratitude. When I am living in self-focused, demanding entitlement, I will find it very hard to be joyful. I will find endless reasons to complain. But if I am living in awe of God's existence, sovereignty, and grace, coupled with a knowledge of the depth of my own need, I will find reasons to be thankful all around me. And as I do, I will live with the constant joy of gratitude.

Or think about peace. Why do I have so much conflict in my life? Why is it easier for me to make war than peace? The answer is simple: I tend to live for myself, and as I do, I find that people are always in my way. But when my motivations change and I am living for God and not for myself, I quit making everything about me. I quit personalizing things that aren't personal. I am willing to overlook minor offenses, and I live in a more peaceful community with others.

How about patience? Do you know why few of us like to wait? We don't like to wait because waiting immediately reminds us that we are not in charge. Nothing more quickly offends our delusions of self-sovereignty than being forced to step out of our own schedules and wait for another. Think about it. You have never gotten angry because you have had to wait for you! Only when my heart is progressively in awe of the agenda of One vastly greater and wiser than me will I surrender my schedule to him and be willing to wait for others.

None of the words in this second portrait pictures a behavior; rather, each represents a character item that will result in a whole catalog of behaviors. And the progressive presence of this kind of character in your life develops in response to the

Holy Spirit's progressive reclaiming of the motivational system of your heart, that is, your capacity for awe. The Spirit works within you to complete the work of Christ so that "those who live might no longer live for themselves" (2 Cor. 5:15). He is working at the deep motivational (awe) level, which is why Paul says that we "have crucified the flesh with its passions and desires" (Gal. 5:24). Yes, your heart was crucified with Christ so that a new heart could live within you. Right here, right now the Holy Spirit who lives inside you is completing that work as he increasingly kills your awe of self and, by grace, plants within you a life-altering awe of God.

You can't do that work of awe reclamation on your own. You desperately need grace. But you and I are called to treasure that work and to pursue and participate in it in any way we can. And we are called to humbly admit our need and again and again run to the grace that stands as our only hope of personal growth and change.

Restoring the proper function to any dysfunctional thing only happens when the power of change is applied to its brokenness. The spiritual growth of progressive sanctification concerns something vastly deeper than a greater allegiance to God's rules. It requires God working to fix what sin has broken, and that brokenness exists in our hearts. Only when awe of God progressively replaces awe of self will we joyfully, willingly, and consistently live as God designed us to live. And for the reclaiming of the motivational system of each of our hearts, we have been given amazing, powerful, zealous, unending, and transformative grace.

10

WORLDVIEW

Who is like you, O LORD, among the gods?
Who is like you, majestic in holiness,
awesome in glorious deeds, doing wonders?
EXODUS 15:11

Comfort, comfort my people, says your God.
Speak tenderly to Jerusalem,
    and cry to her
that her warfare is ended,
    that her iniquity is pardoned,
that she has received from the LORD's hand
    double for all her sins.

A voice cries:
"In the wilderness prepare the way of the LORD;
    make straight in the desert a highway for our God.
Every valley shall be lifted up,
    and every mountain and hill be made low;
the uneven ground shall become level,
    and the rough places a plain.
And the glory of the LORD shall be revealed,
    and all flesh shall see it together,
    for the mouth of the LORD has spoken."

A voice says, "Cry!"
    And I said, "What shall I cry?"

All flesh is grass,
and all its beauty is like the flower of the field.
The grass withers, the flower fades
when the breath of the LORD blows on it;
surely the people are grass.
The grass withers, the flower fades,
but the word of our God will stand forever.

Go on up to a high mountain,
O Zion, herald of good news;
lift up your voice with strength,
O Jerusalem, herald of good news;
lift it up, fear not;
say to the cities of Judah,
"Behold your God!"
Behold, the Lord GOD comes with might,
and his arm rules for him;
behold, his reward is with him,
and his recompense before him.
He will tend his flock like a shepherd;
he will gather the lambs in his arms;
he will carry them in his bosom,
and gently lead those that are with young.

Who has measured the waters in the hollow of his hand
and marked off the heavens with a span,
enclosed the dust of the earth in a measure
and weighed the mountains in scales
and the hills in a balance?
Who has measured the Spirit of the LORD,
or what man shows him his counsel?
Whom did he consult,
and who made him understand?
Who taught him the path of justice,
and taught him knowledge,
and showed him the way of understanding?
Behold, the nations are like a drop from a bucket,

and are accounted as the dust on the scales;
  behold, he takes up the coastlands like fine dust.
Lebanon would not suffice for fuel,
  nor are its beasts enough for a burnt offering.
All the nations are as nothing before him,
  they are accounted by him as less than nothing and emptiness.

To whom then will you liken God,
  or what likeness compare with him?
An idol! A craftsman casts it,
  and a goldsmith overlays it with gold
  and casts for it silver chains.
He who is too impoverished for an offering
  chooses wood that will not rot;
he seeks out a skillful craftsman
  to set up an idol that will not move.

Do you not know? Do you not hear?
  Has it not been told you from the beginning?
  Have you not understood from the foundations of the
    earth?
It is he who sits above the circle of the earth,
  and its inhabitants are like grasshoppers;
who stretches out the heavens like a curtain,
  and spreads them like a tent to dwell in;
who brings princes to nothing,
  and makes the rulers of the earth as emptiness.

Scarcely are they planted, scarcely sown,
  scarcely has their stem taken root in the earth,
when he blows on them, and they wither,
  and the tempest carries them off like stubble.

To whom then will you compare me,
  that I should be like him? says the Holy One.
Lift up your eyes on high and see:
  who created these?

He who brings out their host by number,
  calling them all by name,
by the greatness of his might,
  and because he is strong in power
  not one is missing.

Why do you say, O Jacob,
  and speak, O Israel,
"My way is hidden from the LORD,
  and my right is disregarded by my God"?
Have you not known? Have you not heard?
The LORD is the everlasting God,
  the Creator of the ends of the earth.
He does not faint or grow weary;
  his understanding is unsearchable.
He gives power to the faint,
  and to him who has no might he increases strength.
Even youths shall faint and be weary,
  and young men shall fall exhausted;
but they who wait for the LORD shall renew their strength;
  they shall mount up with wings like eagles;
they shall run and not be weary;
  they shall walk and not faint. (Isaiah 40)

I have never quoted a passage of this length in any book
I have written, but I have a reason for doing it here. I would
like you to do something right now. Go back and read this
quotation of Isaiah 40 two or three times slowly. Let the words
wash over you. Permit the poetic language to paint word pictures in your brain. Give your heart time to absorb the awesome
glory depicted here. As you read, notice how the prophet is
literally stretching the limits of human language to portray for
you the glory of God. Pay attention to how hard he is working
with descriptive words to leave you in heart-pounding, silence-
inducing, worship-stimulating awe of God.

As an author, it is humbling to admit what I am about to admit, but the most important words in this book are words that I have not written. The most important, potentially transformative words in this book were written by the prophet Isaiah as he was inspired by the Holy Spirit. What we need to ask is, "Why were these words given?" and "What are we to do with them now?"

Say Good-bye to "Two-Drawer" Living

Sadly, many people who call themselves Christians live functionally compartmentalized lives. Whether they realize it or not, they have divided their lives neatly into two drawers: *real life* and *spiritual life*.

The *real life* drawer is the one they dig into most and are most comfortable with. It contains all the stuff of everyday life, like job, physical health, food, drink, friends, leisure, money, marriage, parenting, possessions, and daily experiences. This drawer dominates their thinking and their doing. It's where most of their emotional and physical energy is expended and where most of their dreams will be realized or dashed. The big joys they feel and the big sorrows that crush them are usually felt because of what goes on here. This is where they envision the good life for themselves and their children. They often have little functional consciousness of anything other than the mundane stuff that real life throws their way. Yes, they believe in Jesus, his forgiveness, and the eternity to come, but these beliefs don't have a radical impact on the way they think about themselves and life in general. I think I am describing hundreds of thousands of Christians.

They have a second drawer, to be sure. It's the *spiritual life* drawer. All the God stuff goes here. It's the drawer for Sunday services, small group, tithes and offerings, right theology, keeping the rules, short-term missions, and, if they're really spiritual, family worship. Their Christianity is sectored off from the rest of life. Their faith is an aspect of their life, rather than something that shapes everything in their life. And if you pay attention to what's going on with them, you can see clear signs of the negative impact of two-drawer living. We will consider those symptoms after we take a look at why Isaiah 40 was written and then preserved for us.

The "Here's Your God" Worldview

Ask yourself, On any given day, what most influences the way that I think about myself and my life? Isaiah 40 was written to comfort hurting, suffering, and besieged people, but you need to understand the nature of that comfort. This passage should not be relegated to a list of helpful passages for a person needing comfort—along with maxims like "God is sovereign" and "This too will pass." Isaiah 40 is not meant to be an abstract theological salve on the wounds of a hurting person. The reach of Isaiah 40 is meant to be much wider and broader than that. Isaiah 40 is meant to speak into the life of every child of God.

Here's what you need to understand. Isaiah 40 is not comfort literature; it's worldview literature. These words only provide comfort because of the radical, amazing, awe-inspiring worldview that they put forth. When you begin to understand, believe, and live in light of the awesome glory that Isaiah 40 reveals, you have reason to be comforted no matter what you happen to be facing at the moment.

There are two things that Isaiah 40 confronts. It first confronts any view of the world that doesn't place a God of infinite grandeur in the middle of it. You simply cannot properly understand anything unless you look at it through the lens of the awesome glory that Isaiah sticks in your face. Not only does God exist and not only is he active and not only is he in control, but he is also so glorious that it is almost impossible to find words or illustrations that are huge enough to capture his majesty.

I am afraid that a whole lot of functional atheism exists in the church of Jesus Christ. I am afraid that we often live as if there is no God and it's all on us. We tend to worry too much. We tend to control too much. We tend to demand too much. We tend to regret too much. We tend to run after too many God replacements. We do all these things because we so quickly forget God's presence and glory. Isaiah won't let you forget. He arouses your memory with grand and expansive word pictures. He works to reintroduce you to a God you may have forgotten. I can't tell you how many times in counseling I have heard people—people who seem to have a rather well-developed theology—recount their stories but omit God from them entirely. I have thought many times, the fact that they assess their lives in such a God-absent way explains much of the distress, confusion, and despair they are experiencing. They are not discomforted simply because life has been uncomfortable. They are discomforted because they have brought a fundamentally unbiblical worldview to the uncomfortable things they are facing.

But Isaiah 40 addresses a second thing. It addresses the massive number of Christian people who remember God, but the God they remember is small, distant, disconnected, uncaring, and seemingly unwise. In a way, they are suffering not just because of the size of the things they are facing but also because of the smallness of the God they are trusting. Many people have talked to me about God in the middle of difficulties, and after listening to them, I have been struck that, if I believed in the "God" they described, I wouldn't run to him for help either, and I'd be in a panic too.

This is where Isaiah 40 helps us. It addresses an age-old

misconception that you can measure the size and nearness of God by assessing your circumstances. Your idea of God will never be either accurate or stable if you've arrived at it by trying to figure out what he is doing in the situations in your life. This is the mistake that Moses made at the burning bush—as well as the Israelites as they faced the nations on the other side of the Jordan River, and the army of Israel as they faced Goliath and the Philistines, and Gideon as he was called to defeat the Midianites, and the disciples as they hid in fear after Jesus's death. Between the "already" and the "not yet," if you look around, it will seem that the bad guys are winning and that God must lack the power or will to do anything about it.

If you think about it, you can remember times in your life when God confused you, when he seemed distant, or when you couldn't see much evidence of him exercising his power for your welfare. This is precisely why the worldview of Isaiah 40 is so important. It confronts our practical atheism—that is, our conclusions that God is small. It reminds us that proper theology is rooted not in our interpretations of our circumstances but in God's revelation to us of his unchangeable glory. In those moments when we can't see that glory, we need the powerful word pictures of Isaiah 40 to re-form in us an accurate worldview that has an awesome God in the center of it.

Every hope you have as a believer is rooted in the glory of God that Isaiah reveals. Every act of obedience flows out of your belief that One of this awesome grandeur exists. Every courageous act of faith gets its courage from the understanding that this kind of God sits on the throne of the universe. Every bit of personal willingness to persevere through trial is ignited by the remembrance of what Isaiah stretches the words of human language to describe.

So because of this vision, you don't live a two-drawer existence, filing all the real-life things in one drawer and all the spiritual-life things in another. You have only one drawer called *life*. Everything goes in that drawer. Where does Isaiah 40 fit? Well, it's not another drawer. Isaiah 40 is a pair of glasses that you put on so that you can read and understand everything in your life drawer. Only when you wear the glasses of Isaiah 40 can you understand yourself, others, meaning and purpose, right and wrong, identity, morality, history, and the future properly. If awe of God is not at the center of your worldview, you will look at nothing properly.

Now retaining this worldview in a practical manner that actually affects your living presents a struggle. I was thinking this morning of all the duties, responsibilities, opportunities, difficulties, relationships, decisions, and concerns that flood into my mind like a dam that has been breached every morning as I wake up. It's so easy to get distracted by it all. It's so easy to forget things. It's so easy to go through a day without God ever entering your thoughts. It's so easy to load life onto your shoulders and be more motivated by low-grade anxiety than by divine awe. It's so easy to have a formal worldview that is shaped by the theology of the Word of God but has little impact on the way that you act, react, make decisions, or plan.

Perhaps two-drawer living is more natural to us than we would like to think. Perhaps we separate pure lives into real life and spiritual life more than we know. Perhaps the awesome God-reality of Isaiah 40 doesn't invade our consciousness as much as we need it to. Or perhaps what once produced awe in us doesn't do so anymore. That's why Isaiah 40 has been retained for us, because ten out of ten of us will again and again need our awe recharged. We will need to have the distortions in our worldview exposed and cleared out. We will need to remember that in the center of all that makes up our daily existence is a God of expansive, inestimable, awe-inspiring glory. We will need to reconnect with the fact that any world-view that doesn't begin with recognizing this glory distorts reality and is a functional lie. We will need to remember that Isaiah 40 doesn't merely speak to the spiritual dimension of our lives but offers the only lens through which we can see all of life properly. Any other view of life is like looking through carnival glass; the distortions in the glass will warp the appearance of anything you see through it.

The comfort of Isaiah 40 is that it gives us the only world-view that has eternal hope embedded in it. Isaiah 40 comforts us not because it helps us understand life or divine the future but because it reminds us of the glory of the God who rules in majesty over all the things that would otherwise rob us of comfort and hope. We need Isaiah to say to us again and again, "Here is your God!" And we need to let the awesome glory of his description of our God wash our hearts clean of cynicism, doubt, fear, discouragement, anxiety, worry, and control.

Signs of Two-Drawer Living

This has been a very convicting chapter for me to write. As I have been writing, I have been going through one of the most spiritually stressful and discouraging periods of my ministry life. I have tried to make good choices and have failed more than once. I have been under attack by people who loved me. I've had moments when I just wanted to quit. I have thought, "Forget ministry. Forget the church. I just want to go where no one knows me and live a quiet life! I'm tired of trying to help others only to get attacked myself. I'm tired of the burdens and the stress. I'm tired of uncomfortable conversations and tough decisions. I'm tired of private things being made public. I'm tired of praying and praying and nothing changing. In fact, things only seem to get worse. I'm tired of feeling alone and misunderstood."

It is embarrassing to even write these thoughts and feelings down on paper, but they do capture where I've been recently. And it has hit me that, in the past six months, I haven't been very good at preaching the gospel of Isaiah 40 to myself. While I was preaching it to others, I was looking at my ministry life in a way that was lacking the strengthening hope of Isaiah 40. This chapter has reminded me again that it is impossible for me to teach, preach, or write of truths that I don't desperately need myself. If I ever stop being the first audience of my writing, I should stop writing. And as you read this book, please remember me and pray for me. Pray that God will help me to live, with courage and hope, the things that I write.

Now I would like to turn to consider some symptoms of two-drawer living.

1. Anxiety. I am reminded of Christ's question to his followers in Matthew 6, where he essentially asks, "Why are you anxious?" Jesus goes on to propose that it makes sense for the Gentiles (unbelievers) to be anxious because they don't have a heavenly Father. But then turning to his followers, he reminds them that they have a Father who knows what they need and is committed to delivering it to them. Jesus is saying that the anxiety of a believer is directly connected to his street-level view of God. If awe of God does not grip your heart, the anxieties of life will likely influence how you live.

2. Control. Why do we tend to be so controlling? Why do we try to work ourselves into positions of power? Why do we love authority more than we love submitting to authority? Why do we fear the loss of control? Why are we afraid of being controlled? Why do we tend to look at our lives as being out of control? Why do we have to be right, be affirmed, be validated, be respected, or be in power? Why do we not like to be told what to do? Why does control seem to be such a big issue for so many of us?

I am convinced that rest in this chaotic world, submission to authority, and a willingness to give and share power all arise from a certain knowledge that every single detail of our lives is under the careful administration of One of awesome glory. We will rest in the middle of unrest not because we have it figured out but because of who he is. When you are in awe of God's glory, you just don't have to be in control of everything and everyone in your life.

3. Addiction. Why are we so easily addicted to the substances, people, possessions, and experiences in our lives? Why do we tell ourselves that we can control things while the evidence suggests that they are already controlling us? Why is it so hard for us to say "no" to the pleasures of creation? Why do we go back again and again when these things not only fail to deliver what we seek but actually hurt us? Here's the answer: whenever you ask creation to do what only the Creator can do, you are on your way to addiction. You don't get the rest, peace, hope, or life that you're seeking. What you get is a temporary retreat or pleasure or buzz, so you have to go back again and again. Each time, you need a little more, and before long, you are enslaved. When awe of God isn't ruling your heart, you are rendered more susceptible to some kind of addiction.

4. Depression. I do not want to oversimplify this very complex human experience, and I don't want to cheapen the difficulties of people who struggle with depression. But I will say that often one of the spiritual components of the paralyzing darkness of depression is a worldview that has no awesome God in it whatsoever. It's like sitting in a pitch-black basement with no windows and convincing yourself that the sun has ceased to shine, that the world will grow unbearably cold, and that you will die. Your problem is not that the sun has quit shining. If you went upstairs, you would experience its brightness and warmth. Your problem is that, because you can't see its brightness, you allow yourself to think that it has quit shining and that you have no hope. A God-absent view of life surely functions like fertile soil for personal hopelessness.

5. *Debt.* Why do we spend more than we have? Why do we constantly crave more? Why do we envy the affluent? Why are we all too skilled at spending more than we make? Why is it so hard for us to be satisfied with what we have? While I have addressed all these questions in the chapter on materialism, let me speak in summary again. To the degree that you forget the awesome and satisfying glories of the Creator, to that degree you will look for satisfaction in the creation. And because the creation has no ability to satisfy your heart, you will look again and again, acquiring more and more but never achieving contentment of heart.

6. *Fear of man.* Why do we ride the roller coaster of people's responses to us? Why do we fixate on the appreciation of one particular person? Why are we willing to compromise our convictions to get someone to accept us? Why do we rehearse conversations in obsessive regret? Why are we afraid to be honest about our struggles? Why do we live in fear of being known? To the degree that you're getting your identity from the people around you and not from the awesome God of Isaiah 40, to that degree you will be a sitting duck for fear of man.

7. *Workaholism.* Why do we work longer and harder than we should responsibly work? Why are we focused on achievement and obsessed with success? Why are we willing to sacrifice family and friendships to get ourselves a few rungs further up the ladder of achievement? Why do position and power tend to

mean too much to us? Again, if you need a public track record of personal success to have inner rest and peace, rather than getting your peace from your connection to the glorious God of Isaiah 40, you will tend to work more than you should.

8. Dissatisfaction. Perhaps all the moans and groans of dashed dreams and discontented hearts that color our thoughts and conversations expose the degree to which the glory that we say we believe in (Isaiah 40) gets separated from the way that we think about and live our everyday lives. Maybe we're dissatisfied not just because people are unpredictable and life is hard. Perhaps we're experiencing two-drawer dissatisfaction. Perhaps the strengthening rest that is depicted at the end of Isaiah 40 has eluded us because the awesome God of Isaiah 40 is not in our thoughts and at the center of the way we make sense of our life (worldview).

So pray right now that God would grace you with the desire and strength to get yourself up out of that dark basement and into the comforting and encouraging light of his existence and glory, and believe that you can fly. Not because you understand, are appreciated, or are in control, but because God controls all things, because he is glorious, and because by grace he is all that he is for you.

11

CHURCH

If you don't feel strong desires for the manifestation of the glory of God, it is not because you have drunk deeply and are satisfied. It is because you have nibbled so long at the table of the world. Your soul is stuffed with small things, and there is no room for the great.

JOHN PIPER [9]

Put on then, as God's chosen ones, holy and beloved, compassionate hearts, kindness, humility, meekness, and patience, bearing with one another and, if one has a complaint against another, forgiving each other; as the Lord has forgiven you, so you also must forgive. And above all these put on love, which binds everything together in perfect harmony. And let the peace of Christ rule in your hearts, to which indeed you were called in one body. And be thankful. Let the word of Christ dwell in you richly, teaching and admonishing one another in all wisdom, singing psalms and hymns and spiritual songs, with thankfulness in your hearts to God. And whatever you do, in word or deed, do everything in the name of the Lord Jesus, giving thanks to God the Father through him. (Col. 3:12–17)

Jim said that he and Sherri will never forget driving onto the campus of First Baptist Church (FBC). The grounds and the building were a picture of longevity and stability. FBC had been founded almost two hundred years earlier and had remained faithful to the gospel throughout its storied history. The huge, beautiful, and traditional sanctuary made Jim and Sherri feel safe and secure. They loved the regal worship service and the elegant preaching. But within their first year at FBC, they both began feeling smothered by tradition. Sherri told Jim she just couldn't go to a church that was so traditional that you felt embarrassed if you coughed during the worship service.

A friend had told Sherri about the Vine, so they gave it a try. "What a breath of fresh air!" Sherri exclaimed after their first visit; attending the Vine wasn't a hard decision for them at all. After all the traditionalism of FBC, they liked the warehouse environment and the rather raucous worship. Jim thought the preaching was creative, almost conversational. He told Sherri it was much easier to listen to than the theological lectures at FBC. But before long, the preaching began to drive Jim and Sherri crazy. The rambling style, marked with a heavy dose of humor, started to irk them, so they began to look again.

They found Fleet Street Presbyterian Church almost by accident. It was a block away from a restaurant they tried one Friday night, and the only place to park was right in front of the church. They decided to give Fleet Street a shot. That first Sunday they thought they had found the best of both worlds. The service included some traditional elements in a more traditional setting, but the congregation was young, the music was lively, and the pastor had a very contemporary way of communicating biblical truth. At the same time, as they began attending Fleet Street, Jim and Sherri started experiencing some bumps in their marriage. They were happy to see that Fleet Street had a well-developed counseling ministry, so they sought help for their marriage. But after two sessions, Jim was so upset by the counsel they received that he said he not only lost all confidence in his counselor but also refused to attend a church that would promote that kind of "help."

Jim and Sherri learned about Immanuel, a little church plant, through a flyer they received in the mail. They had no other options, so they thought they would give it a try. The first Sunday was very uncomfortable because only about sixty people were there. It felt like they were attending someone else's family reunion. But the people were very friendly, and they decided to go back. Just as Jim and Sherri were beginning to think that Immanuel would work for them, their teenage children began to protest. Emma and Josh hated the church because only one other teenager attended. They both said they couldn't understand why their parents would choose a church that had nothing for them. With reluctance, and without a plan, Jim and Sherri left Immanuel.

Jim and Sherri now go to a megachurch about twice a month. They love that they can slip in and out without being noticed, and they have no intention of joining. Their children reluctantly go with them on Sunday morning but express no interest whatsoever in the church's youth ministry. Jim says they would leave this church in a second if they could find a better alternative, but they're tired of looking.

Now go back and read the verses that open this chapter again and reflect on your personal relationship to your local church. Think about how your church approaches its ministry. Consider the expectations your church has for you. Colossians 3:12–17 puts before us a radical, countercultural view of what God designed the church to be and do. It is a singeing critique of the passive relationship that most believers have to the church to which they have for the moment committed themselves. (Because this is such a pressing issue, I plan to make an extended unpacking of Colossians 3 the topic of a future book.)

Why do so many Christians act like Jim and Sherri? Why aren't most Christians living the local church lifestyle captured by these words in Colossians 3? Why do so many of us think of church as something we attend rather than a central mission of our lives? Why do we most often expect the paid church staff to shoulder almost the entire burden of ministry? Why don't more of us share Paul's understanding of what the church is? Why aren't more believers trained and ready for the ministry to which God has called them? What is at the root of Jim and Sherri's struggle with the church?

The answers to these questions are embedded in the opening words of Colossians 3: "If then you have been raised with Christ, seek the things that are above, where Christ is, seated at the right hand of God. Set your minds on things that are above, not on things that are on earth" (Col. 3:1–2). The radical ecclesiastical lifestyle of Colossians 3:12–17 will never happen until God first radically recaptures your heart, as these verses depict.

Understanding the State of Things

A shocking amount of Christian consumerism exists in the church of Jesus Christ today. Many, many believers think of their church as a place to attend rather than something with which they are intimately involved. They think of church as a worship gathering, a weekly duty that is part of the religious dimension of their lives. It is sad, but most pastors seem content with an ever-increasing attendance, enough financial giving to fuel church programs, and a small percentage of people who will volunteer in episodic ministry. In most churches, the paid staff carry the burden of the church's spiritual health, while the members happily play their role as the recipients.

People move from church to church as if the churches in

their community are nothing more than ecclesiastical department stores. They're shopping for just the right preacher, women's ministry, youth ministry, or worship style. These Christians' relationship to the church mirrors my relationship to Macy's. If I go to Macy's looking for a certain color and style shirt and they don't have it, I feel no guilt whatsoever in leaving Macy's and going to look for it at Bloomingdale's. I move from store to store until I find what I want because my commitment is not to a particular store but to myself and the satisfaction of my desire for that shirt.

Hordes of Christians have this kind of church lifestyle, and they will, like shoppers, chase the deal of the moment. Maybe that's running after the celebrity preacher, the cool Saturday night worship band, or the best youth program ever. They are high-expectation and low-commitment attenders, and there is a good possibility that they will soon be worshiping somewhere different from where they are right now.

Many Christians also live inside the church virtually unknown. They slip in and out of the weekly service almost unnoticed. Sure, they will exchange niceties with the people near them, and if they do that, they will learn a few cursory details about one another's lives, but they don't really have a relationship with the people with whom they worship. Most of what they call fellowship simply isn't. It seldom reaches deeper than the kind of conversation you would have at the local pub. I think we should just be honest and call it "pubship." Many Christians live in a Christian community where no one knows the condition of their marriage, their struggles as parents, or the places where they feel overburdened and overwhelmed. No one knows what goes on in the private moments of their lives, where they are defeated by temptation again and again or where they are tempted to doubt the goodness of God. Their life in the church is not the life of an essential member of an organic body of faith where each member feels the pain when another member hurts. No, they are spiritual shoppers looking for the best religious store in town.

Even more believers have no personal commitment to ministry. Sure, they put a little money in the plate to pay for professional staff to shoulder ministry, but they don't live with a ministry mentality. To them, ministry is a formal religious thing conceived, programmed, and scheduled by their church. In this view, if you get involved in ministry, you step out of your life for a moment of ministry and then back into your life. Here ministry interrupts the regular routine, representing an exceptional thing for the spiritually zealous. How many believers really live a lifestyle that results from believing that God has graced them to be not just *recipients* of the work of his kingdom but *instruments* of the work of the kingdom as well? When you believe this, you live with a constant ministry mentality that results in an everyday ministry lifestyle. Here ministry is no interruption but an essential part of the normal routine.

Many more Christians than we would imagine have attached their Christianity to their pursuit of the "American dream." Whether they know it or not, they have bought into the cultural definition of success, and they are pursuing the culture's portrait of the "good life": career success, financial ease, the big house, the trendy wardrobe, the fancy food, and the extravagant vacations. And because they are, they spend most of their physical, emotional, and spiritual energy gaining, maintaining, keeping, and enjoying these things, rather than investing in the eternal treasures of the kingdom of God through the vehicle of their local church. Sadly, the cultural dream is their vocation, and their Christianity is relegated to a religious pastime.

You have to ask yourself, why? Why has this become the

regular state of things? Why do so many Christians have such a passive relationship to the church?

And Now for Our Passage

When it comes to the church, Colossians 3 presents to us a *radical lifestyle* that results from a *commitment of the heart*. Let's look at the radical lifestyle first. This lifestyle is rooted in an understanding of what I have called in another book God's "total involvement paradigm."[10] What does this mean? It means God has designed that all his people would be involved in his redemptive work all the time. It means no one is given grace just to be a recipient but to be an instrument of that very same grace in the lives of others. This passage highlights five characteristics of this radical ministry lifestyle to which God has called each of us. If you are committed to this lifestyle you will do the following:

1. Take your local-church relationships seriously (vv. 12–14). These verses list several character qualities—compassion, kindness, humility, meekness, patience, forbearance, forgiveness—and God expects every believer to commit to nurturing these qualities in all their relationships. They form the bedrock of this ministry lifestyle, and they immediately confront us with the fact that God owns our relationships—we do not—and that he has a higher purpose for them than we do.

If we were honest, I think most of us would have to admit that we rarely look at our everyday relationships with a ministry mentality. We tend to view our relationships as little more than containers for our personal happiness. When you have a personal-happiness agenda for your relationships, four things will tend to happen: (1) You will turn moments of ministry into moments of anger, seeing another person's sin or need as an interruption or hassle rather than an opportunity for grace. (2) You will tend to do this because you will personalize what is not personal. You will make it all about you when, in actuality, that person has in no way plotted against you. Rather, God has chosen to reveal their need to you so you can be his tool of grace. (3) Because you've personalized what is not personal, you will likely become adversarial in your response. It won't be you for them but you against them because they are in the way of something you want. (4) And finally, you will settle for quick situational solutions that don't really bring God's grace to the heart of the matter. You will strike back or walk away, but you won't be a tool in God's hands.

God intends these character qualities to transform the relationships of your daily life, changing them from containers for your happiness to workrooms for the transforming grace of the Redeemer.

2. Rest in the peace of the gospel (v. 15). Why does Paul call for the "peace of Christ" to rule in our hearts? Well, that phrase is a hint that he is first talking about something more foundational than relational peace. We must first have the peace of Christ if you and I are ever going to experience lasting peace in the community around us. Why peace of Christ? Because this rest for the heart only comes when you are getting your identity and personal security from the gospel of the Lord Jesus Christ. Because you rest in his forgiveness, you don't need to fear being exposed since nothing could be known about you that hasn't already been covered by his sacrificial work. Because you rest in his acceptance, you are freed from riding the roller coaster of people's responses to you. Because you rest in his indwelling power, you are not afraid of the difficulties and challenges of personal ministry. You see, the gospel frees you from focusing so much on yourself that you have little time to minister to others.

3. Be a committed student of God's Word (v. 16). It is my experience that most Christians are barely biblically literate, let alone equipped to use their Bible appropriately and effectively in personal ministry. When you don't know your Bible well, you will tend to use it as an isolated collection of wisdom statements for daily living, and you will tend to look for the verse that best seems to fit the situation you are discussing. This method completely misses the genius of the Bible's grand redemptive themes that form the basis of the hope and courage of the brand-new way of living to which God has called us. Or a second thing will happen, and sadly, I think this happens very often: ministry opportunities will tend to devolve into human advice giving. Because we don't know God's Word well, we will dip into our own experience and tell people what we think they should do, ignoring God's call to them, his grace in them, and his wisdom for them.

4. Look for ministry opportunities (v. 16). Paul says you need the Word of God dwelling in you richly so that you are ready to "teach" and "admonish." Think about these two words. They tend to be ministry terms that we apply only to formally trained, full-time, paid ministry staff. Yet Paul is saying here that these two words capture God's call to every believer. For the church to be the church—not just a place where you can find ministry but where the people are a ministering community—every believer must accept his or her role in the life of every other believer. It may sound radical, but it is God's plan that all of his children would teach and all of his children would admonish. What does this mean? What does this look like? To teach means that I am always committed and ready when God gives me the opportunity to help others see life from God's perspective. And to admonish means that I am always committed and ready when God gives me the opportunity to help others see themselves in the mirror of God's Word. No church will ever be able to afford enough staff to cover all the teaching and admonishing moments that God will give his church in any given week.

5. Recognize that your life no longer belongs to you (v. 17). Here again is a reminder to do everything in God's name. We have no separate, private lives that belong to us. God owns us, and he owns every one of our relationships. A lifestyle of ministry begins with a surrender to the ownership of the Lord over all we are and all we have.

So why don't more Christians live this way? The answer is found in the words noted earlier that I will repeat here: "Set your minds on things that are above, not on things that are on earth" (Col. 3:2). This sentence really does yank us back to the core message of this book. It takes us back to the fundamental struggle that rages in my heart and yours, which is why I decided to write what you now have in your hands.

Here's what we all need to understand. The church (by which I mean the people, not the institution) doesn't first have a people-mobilization problem or a people-training problem. The church of Jesus Christ has an awe problem. It's not that the church is losing the ministry war; it is losing the awe war. And because it is losing the awe war, very few people participate in very much ministry.

Let me give you a practical example and then explain it. I have been convinced for a long time that evangelism classes don't produce evangelists. Evangelism classes are a way of training people who are already committed to an evangelistic lifestyle. Without that commitment, the class won't turn you into an evangelist. Counseling training doesn't produce counselors. It can simply impart necessary understanding and skills to people who are already committed to a lifestyle of personal ministry.

So Colossians 3:2 goes right to the heart of the matter, which happens to be the heart. It addresses what has captured the awe capacity of your heart. Remember, your heart always functions in the awe of something. The thoughts, desires, motivations, purposes, and choices of your heart are all shaped by whatever your heart is in awe of. This passage simplifies this profound struggle down to two possible options. Either your heart lives in a fundamental, life-shaping awe of the horizontal, physical, created world ("things that are on the earth"), or your heart lives in a foundational vertical awe of God, his work, his grace, and his kingdom.

If your heart has been captured by the glories of the physical world's people, places, experiences, and things, that's where you will invest the majority of your physical, emotional, and spiritual energies. And because you are seeking to find true happiness and fulfillment here, your relationship to your church and its work and to your community with other believers will exist as an adjunct, or add-on, to what your life is really about. I think hundreds of thousands of believers live this way. Yes, they are God's children. Yes, they have been redeemed by his blood and accepted by his grace. But to them, church is a place that they attend thankfully but that constitutes no essential aspect of their living.

Yet if your heart is being progressively captured by the awe of God, his work, his grace, and his kingdom ("things that are above"), you will see your church not just as a place you attend but as a major commitment of your life, and you will live with a ministry lifestyle in the place where God has put you. When awe of God has captured your heart, ministry will fill your schedule. You won't need the church to schedule ministry for you; you will approach work, marriage, parenting, extended family, friendships, and community with a ministry mentality. Awe of God will free you from thinking of your life as belonging to you and of ministry as temporarily offering pieces of your life to God that you will quickly take back as an episode of ministry ends. Awe means that you will look at everything in your life through the lens of God's existence and glory, and you will surrender all your life to his purpose, humbly recognizing that, when you do this, you are not offering what is yours to him but returning what he already owns back to him for his use.

If the church is populated with people who have set their minds on the things that are on earth, then the bulk of people in the church will have a passive relationship to the church, and the burden of ministry will fall on the shoulders of a few paid staffers. But if the church is populated with people who have set their minds on things above, then widespread daily ministry will take place in the hallways, bedrooms, boardrooms, family rooms, and vans of everyday life. There is a direct connection between what kind of awe has captured your heart and the amount of ministry that occupies your life.

If you have read this chapter and thought, "Paul, I'm one of those passive people," don't be paralyzed by guilt and regret. No, run to your Redeemer. Confess what has ruled your heart, and cry out for his delivering and enabling grace. And as you do, remember once again that your Lord will never turn a deaf ear to the cries of one of his children. You too can experience a rejuvenated awe of God that issues forth in a ministry mindset that will transform your church relationships.

12

PARENTING

A man can no more diminish God's glory by refusing to worship Him than a lunatic can put out the sun by scribbling the word 'darkness' on the walls of his cell.

C. S. LEWIS[11]

If you had to capture on a piece of paper what God's job description of the family is, what would you write? What has God called parents to be and to do? What goals should you have for your children? When you're at the end of a week as a parent and you say, "That was a good week," what makes you say that? What are you trying to accomplish with all those early-morning and late-night conversations? What are you trying to produce with all those mini-lectures? What are you trying to instill in your children when you seek to bring peace to all those sibling wars? If you had to paint a portrait of the ideal child you're trying to produce, what would that portrait look like? How will you know when you have been successful?

We all know that few things in life are as profoundly important as being God's agent for forming a human soul. But I fear that many of us parent without a big picture, without a grand agenda in mind. We seem to lack expansive goals that guide everything we do as parents. We do various things with the hope that our children will behave, will be polite, and will believe, but our parenting tends to be piecemeal and reactive rather than unified around a central vision or an overarching goal.

Judy was a frustrated parent, and in her frustration, she reached out to me. She had begun to hate her relationship with her children. No, she didn't hate her children; what she hated was the negative cast of her relationship with them. Judy said, "All I am is a lawgiver, a prosecutor, a judge, a jury, and a jailer. From morning to night, I say no over and over again and enforce punishments when my children don't respond. I am always wondering what they're going to do next, and they see me coming and wonder what they've done wrong. I know I must be missing something, but I just don't know what it is."

Sally and Bill approached me at a parenting conference. Sally was in tears before she spoke. She told me that it was embarrassing to have to admit what she was about to admit, but she had to talk to someone. Sally proceeded to tell me that she had no ability whatsoever to control her four-year-old. "Rather than me parenting him, he controls me," she said sadly. She expressed that she was already scared to death as she thought of what it would be like when her son became a teenager.

Frank shared with me the grief of thousands of fathers. He had been a conscious and faithful disciplinarian. While they were at home, his kids all submitted to his authority. In many ways, at school, church, home, and work, Frank's children looked like model kids. People in Frank's church repeatedly told him what a fine job he had done as a father. Frank confessed that when his first son graduated from high school at the top of his class, he was not just proud of his son, he was proud of himself. But as he stood before me, Frank didn't look like a proud and self-confident father. He looked broken and defeated. "I thought we did it all right, but when my son and daughter went away to college, they both forsook the faith. They have no relationship with God and little closeness with us."

I can't tell you how many of these conversations I've had with parents over the years. The names and places differ, but the themes are all the same. Masses of Christian parents have lost their way or never had their way in the first place. Thousands of parents have begun to think that all their hard work has been for naught. Thousands of parents don't know what they're doing or why they're doing what they're doing. Thousands of good-hearted, hard-working parents lack the big picture that would give sense and direction to everything they do. This chapter addresses what is missing in the parenting of countless well-meaning believers. Let's begin by examining the "state of the union."

Parenting without the Big Picture

I am convinced after talking with hundreds of parents that most parents lack a big, overarching vision that guides all that they do with their children. Sure, they want their children to believe in Jesus, and they want their children to obey, and they hope that they will have athletic and musical ability along with a good education, marriage, and career. But at the street level, they're just reacting to whatever comes at them on a particular day. Yes, they may say and do many good things with their children. Yes, they are sincere about their children's spiritual life. And yes, they work to enforce a set of rules to shape their children's behavior. But it is a reactive system.

The problem with reactive parenting is that it lacks a big picture, which enables parents to interpret what is going on in the hearts and lives of their children and thus target the significant heart issues that are really the focus of all good and successful parenting. This inadequate vision leaves these parents with a neat system set up to control, regulate, and conform the behavior of their children. Now if all you do is control the behavior of your children when they are in the home with you, then when they leave your home, they will have nothing. When they leave home and no longer have that system of control over them, their lives will go where their heart has been for a long time.

Let me give you an example. Every year thousands of supposedly Christian young people go off to residential universities and forsake the faith. I would propose to you that they are not forsaking the faith at all. They never had it in the first place. They grew up under a system of control that forced the faith upon them, but when they get to college and the system vanishes, their true hearts reveal themselves.

Reactive parenting has another problem. Since it lacks a grand, big vision, it tends to be way more determined on any given day by the emotion or mood of the parent. The thing that was okay yesterday is not okay today because mom isn't doing well. Or the thing that made dad angry yesterday doesn't seem to bother him at all today. Instead of children being molded by a consistent standard, they become emotional weathermen, reading the "weather" of their parents to see what they can or cannot get away with. Siblings will even have conversations to find out if one or the other is cued into how their parents are doing on any given day.

This is simply not the way that God intended children to be parented. It becomes an emotionally driven, behavior-control system that misses both the centrality of the heart and the transforming power of the gospel to create lasting change in the child's behavior.

The Big Picture

Here's what every parent needs to understand: your child doesn't just have a behavior problem; he or she has a heart problem.

The Bible teaches that all the words and behavior of a child are controlled, shaped, and directed by what's in that child's heart (see Luke 6:43–45). And the core dysfunction of the heart of every child doesn't first have to do with *law*; it has to do with *awe*. Every child is born with a heart controlled more by awe of self than by awe of God.

Let me say it this way: every child comes into the world embracing two very seductive but equally seductive lies. First is the lie of *autonomy*. Autonomy says, "I am an independent human being, and I have a right to live my life the way I want to live it." Those early battles that you have with your child about what to eat, what to wear, and when to go to sleep are not just about those issues. Your child is pushing back because your child does not want to be ruled. She sees herself in the center of her universe. He has appointed himself as a little self-sovereign. Although they have no understanding of a healthy human diet, what is appropriate to wear when, and the amount of sleep a healthy child requires, they will fight you because they do not want to be told what to do. That's why a little boy will scream "no!" at an adult four times his size or a little girl will stiffen up in anger and turn red. They're after autonomy. They want no other authority over them than their own.

The second lie is the lie of *self-sufficiency*. This lie says, "I have everything I need inside myself to be what I am supposed to be and to do what I am supposed to do." Although young children have almost no understanding of the world around them, they will resist help because they want to hold onto the delusion that they do not need wisdom, instruction, or correction. Let me give you an example. Little Jimmy has discovered that his shoes have laces, and he has realized that after he puts the shoes on, they need to be tied. So you walk into Jimmy's bedroom, and he has his shoes on the wrong feet and is fumbling with the laces.

You know that he could fumble with those laces for a century and not make a bow, but when you bend down to assist him, he slaps away your hand. He wants to believe that he is capable, that he doesn't need to be quiet, submit, and learn.

These two lies were first told by the Serpent in the garden of Eden and unleashed an unspeakable chain of disastrous consequences on the physical world and on humanity. Now it's important to understand that these laws reveal that your child has not only a law problem, which he or she does, but a deeper and more formative awe problem. Children will only live as God has ordained them to live if their hearts have been freed from their bondage to awe of self and have been captured by the awe of God.

So, parents, it simply doesn't work to have a law system as the model for your parenting. Now maybe you're thinking, "But don't my children need rules and enforcement in their lives? Don't they need constant authority?" Of course they do, but these things are not enough. If all your children needed was a tight system of law to be what they're supposed to be and to do what they're supposed to do, Jesus would never have had to come and live a perfect life, shed his precious blood, and rise again from the grave. The gospel of Jesus Christ tells us that this kind of parenting simply is not enough.

Do your children need the law? Yes, they do! God employs the law to help your children see how spiritually needy they are. The law tells your children how God wants them to live, but the law can never, ever deliver them from the sin and self-worship that have captured their hearts.

So our parenting must target the central heart issue of our children. We know that as long as their hearts are ruled by awe of self, they will push against our authority, they will go their own way, and they will practically ignore the God who created and sustains them. This means that our parenting must be guided by a great big awe agenda. We need to do everything we can to put the glory of God and his grace before our children so that the awe of God would rule over their hearts.

Now maybe you're thinking, "Paul, how in the world do we do that?" I'm afraid that for many of us, the only time we regularly refer to God as parents is when our children will not listen to us, and so we get God out as the ultimate threat. "You know, God is watching, and he could crush you like a bug!" This just makes the hearts of children want to run away from such a God!

Well, God in his condescending love and mercy has helped us here because he has created his world in such a way that it would reveal him. The fact that the physical world points to God is no accident; it was his divine intention as he was forming the physical universe with his awesome power. So God has made his power, faithfulness, wisdom, goodness, love, and mercy visible to us every day through the lens of the world that he created. Every glorious created thing points to a God of far greater glory. So, parents, it's not unnatural to talk about God every day to your children; it's positively unnatural not to. God made hot, and God made cold. God made water that freezes on one end and boils on the other (wow!). God made the delicacy of a lily, the inexhaustible wings of a hummingbird, the lumbering gait of an elephant, the multicolored stripes of a rainbow, the terror of a storm, the processes of the earth to supply us food to eat, the splash of stars at night, and a myriad of other things to see, hear, touch, and taste every day. You just can't get up in the morning without bumping into God. Every day it's God here, God there, God over there and there and there.

Now, parents, you need to understand something further. You are parenting children who have a perverse ability to look at the world around them and not see God. Sin and self blind the eyes of your children to the glory everywhere around them, the glory that has the power to change their hearts and put them in their proper place. They see the tree, but they don't see the glory. They taste the sumptuous meal, but they don't see the awesome God who made everything they just enjoyed. They may be afraid of the storm, but they have little fear of the power of the One who sent it. The disaster of spiritual blindness is one of the reasons God put you on earth and in the lives of your children. He has strategically positioned you so that you would function as his instruments of seeing, pointing to his presence, power, and glory over and over every day. He has called you to be a tool that recaptures the awe of your children's hearts, so that awe of him would reign where awe of self once did. You can nurture that change as a result of his grace, but you are called to commit yourself to being a tool of his awe-recapturing agenda (see Psalm 145).

So when you go to the petting zoo with your little girl, talk about the God who made each distinct characteristic of every single animal. When you bake bread, talk about how the rising of dough is just one of millions of physical, chemical processes that came out of the mind of God. When your child smells a fragrant flower, talk about how God created these smells and then gave us the organs in our body to take them in and enjoy them. When you're hiking with your son through the woods, talk about the One who created these huge organisms with arms that reach toward the heavens. When your child is sick, talk about the One who created all the delicate, interdependent systems of the body that must work in complete harmony for us to be well. When your daughter is complaining about the rainy weather, talk about what an impossible job it would be to control the world's weather, yet God does it every day. Have your young son make faces in the mirror, and talk about how God designed all those little muscles in the face that allow us to communicate so much without saying a word. I could give page after page of illustration after illustration. We live in the middle of an awesome, never-ending glory display, and it is our job—and should be our joy—to point our children to this glory again and again day after day.

But here's the rub. In parenting it is very hard to give away what you don't have. In many of our homes, it's not just our children who are blind to the awesome display of God's presence, power, and glory everywhere around us; *we* are also blind to it. So perhaps we should start with asking God not to open our children's eyes, but first to open ours, so that we can help them to see. It is impossible to point someone to something that you don't see. We tend to see transportation that needs to be supplied, lunches that need to be made, clothes that need to be washed, activities that need to be scheduled, homework that needs to be done, and sibling squabbles that need to be resolved. For some of us, we can go through days with no awareness of God whatsoever. Only as God graciously opens our eyes to his glory and captures our hearts with his awe will we ever be his instruments in the eyes of our children.

Maybe you're saying to yourself right now, "But I just want to have children who obey and do what is right." So what is the only pathway to complete and willing submission to God's authority and his law? Only when our children are living out of a heartfelt awe of God will they quit living for themselves, recognize God's authority, and submit to the instruments of his authority that God has placed in their lives—their parents. Only awe of God has the power to defeat awe of self in my heart. It's the glory of God that can protect our children from the seductive draw of self-glory. If awe doesn't rule my child's heart,

God's law won't control my child's behavior. The great battle of parenting is not the battle of behavior; it's the battle for what kind of awe will rule children's hearts.

Let's get even more specific. Parents, you don't have any independent authority over your children. None. Your children haven't been given to you as indentured servants to make your life easier. They have not been given to build your identity or prop up your reputation. They are not to be viewed as potential trophies on the mantel of your success. The only kind of authority you have is representative or ambassadorial authority.

Here's God's plan: God intends to make his invisible authority visible in the lives of children through their parents, who exercise their authority in submission to him. Parents, there is no higher calling than this. You have been chosen to visibly represent the authority of God on earth in the lives of your children. You are the look on God's face. You are the tone of his voice. You are the touch of his hand. You are his character and attitude. This means that every time you exercise authority in the lives of your children, it must be a beautiful picture of the patient, firm, gracious, wise, loving, tender, merciful, forgiving, and faithful authority of God. Why? Because your job is to leave your children in awe of the stunning, rescuing beauty of God's authority. Your job is to be used of God to help your children move from natural rebels against any authority but their own to those who are in awe of God's authority. Once they embrace this awe of God, they will cheerfully submit to his rules and honor the visible representatives of his authority whom God has placed in their lives.

This means that every time your authority is exercised in a selfish, impatient, irritable, name-calling, abusive, partial, or condemning way, you are not part of what God is doing in the life of your child; you are in the way of it. When you express your authority this way, you don't lead your children to stand in awe of the beauty and helpfulness of God's authority. No, you help deepen the natural rebellion your child has toward it. You know that when anyone has gotten up in your face and ripped into you, you have never felt thankful, loved, or helped. That has never made you feel rescued and cared for. In those situations, you have never felt like you're being blessed with rare wisdom. No, you just want the pain of the demeaning onslaught to end. You see, if my child has an awe problem in his heart and I have been sent to visibly represent the God who should be at the center of his awe capacity, then the manner in which I respond to my child affects the way he views God himself.

Who can read what I have just written and say, "No problem, I can do that!" If you have any humility and sanity as a parent, you would confess with me that you are not up to such a task. You are unworthy of such a high calling. I know I can be so incredibly impatient, so easily irritated, so comfortable with failing. Yet when God's grace has produced in me greater awe of him than I have for myself, I will then be motivated to serve as an instrument of awe of him in the lives of my children. This means not only that my children need parenting that rescues their awe but that I need that as well. I need a heavenly Father who will again and again show me his glory until this fickle heart of mine rests in an awe-filled understanding that he is the only One worthy of the worship of my heart.

What, then, is the fruit of the awe of God in the hearts of our children? I would propose to you that awe of God can produce in the heart of a child what every parent longs for. A child whose heart is ruled by the awe of God will submit to authority, will listen to and value wisdom, and will not resist but will hunger for rescue and will surrender control to God and the ambassadors he has placed in his life.

You and I can't recapture the hearts of our children; only God can. But we need to understand that this is the mission he has called us to be part of. We need to recognize the daily evidence that our children live out of an attitude and behavior-shaping awe of self. And we need to do everything we can to point to God's visible glory, so that the hearts of our children will, by grace, be captured by awe of him. We need to finally realize that it is not enough to announce and enforce God's law; we should carry out both of these charges, but we must also do more. And we must submit our parenting to the reality that only when our children are in awe of God will they surrender their lives to his control, heed the call of his Word, and esteem the authorities that he has graciously placed over them. To do this, we also need to be rescued by his grace, rescued not from our children but from the selfishness and pride of our own hearts. Thankfully, Jesus purchased this rescue.

WORK

*Let all the earth fear the L*ORD*;*
let all the inhabitants of the world stand in awe of him!
PSALM 33:8

John is never at home. Jenny, his wife, has gotten used to having dinner alone with the kids and making excuses for John's absence at all the evening activities she attends by herself.

To say that Frank is driven and aggressive would be the understatement of the century. He has left a trail of bodies behind him as he has climbed the corporate ladder.

Gina has been in a significant depression since her firm downsized and permanently furloughed her. She can barely get out of bed in the morning and says she feels like her life is over.

Bill can't believe that he makes as much as he makes. He never imagined he would experience such affluence, yet he is still deeply in debt.

Sharon says that she has never been satisfied with any job she has ever had because she is always able to spot one that appears more exciting and challenging.

Both Sam and Freda work sixty hours a week. They have little free time to enjoy their beautiful home, and they have always had to hire help to care for their children.

Peter keeps saying that when he reaches a certain level of success, he will cut back and get more involved with the ministries of his church, but even as his success exceeds his goals, church involvement never happens.

Tim had a dream of owning his own business, a dream he finally achieved. That business demands his attention 24/7, and his wife and children feel his absence daily.

Sean hasn't taken a vacation in years. He says he wants to, but he just can't seem to break free from his duties to do it.

Sally lost her job, and when she did, she lost her desire to ever have a job again. She feels guilty that she is not working but not guilty enough to do something about it.

Jose learned to value hard work at the feet of his father, but even though he works constantly, he has little to show for it.

Mike is the boss but not the kind that employees love. He is known for being endlessly demanding and seldom encouraging, and his business has suffered from a constant turnover of employees.

Kim told Tom, her pastor-husband, that he should just put a bed in his office because he's never at home.

Can I be so bold as to ask, what's going on with your world of work? Is your life of work balanced appropriately? Do spiritual and relational commitments suffer because of your job? Could it be that you're asking work to do for you what it cannot do? How often do you feel torn between the demands of work and the responsibilities of family?

Work and the Limits of Time

People often propose that workaholics have a "priorities" problem, and while I understand that, I don't find that critique specific or deep enough. Often people are counseled to list their priorities from top to bottom, and making such a list may be helpful for gaining insight, but it simply doesn't lead to a solution. Let me suggest two reasons why.

First, none of us lives "listologically." By that I mean that you don't list your priorities and then get up every day and start at the top of the list again. Everything on the list is important in some way, and nothing on the list can be responsibly ignored. Your life is simply not a list of priorities but rather the coming together of three inescapable dimensions of calling. You are called to *relationships*, you are called to *work*, and you are called to *God*. Each of these is a significant expression of how God calls every one of us to live. In a way, none of them is more important than the other since each exists because of divine calling. So rather than a list, you have three intersecting, overlapping domains of godly living: the social domain, the labor domain, and the spiritual domain (although everything is spiritual). Think of these as a triad of overlapping circles, where each circle connects with the other two.

Yet you have a limited amount of time to devote to these domains—24 hours in a day, 7 days in a week, 30 days in a month, and 365 days in a year. So if one activity expands over a longer span of time, it can only expand because you have contracted the duration of another activity. Almost no one says, "Work is a greater priority to me than family, so I am going to put family lower on my list." Rather, the demands of work gradually begin to gobble up more and more of my time, and as they do, because I don't have limitless time, I am left with less time for my family. Few believers would say that work is more important than their relationships with God and his people, but their life of work expands to the point where they have little time left to do anything but casually attend the church to which they once committed themselves. It is impossible for one area of my calling to expand without it causing other areas of equally important calling to contract. So it's important to ask not what your priorities are but if your world of work has expanded to the point that it has caused a harmful contraction of your time with your family and your pursuit of God? This seems to me to be a much more helpful way of thinking about the schedule tensions that so many of us experience when it comes to work, family, and church.

Second, listing your priorities doesn't get at causality. The question we need to ask and answer is, why are so many of us closet workaholics? Why are so many of us so driven when it comes to our careers? Why are so many of us working to the detriment of family and church? Why do so many successful Christians carry around with them marital and parental guilt? Why is it so hard for us to keep work in its proper, God-designed place?

Work and Identity

I want to say what I have said again and again in this book, but in a different way. I don't think that the workaholics among us have first a priorities or a schedule problem; I think that they have an awe problem, which results in a relationally and spiritually detrimental schedule problem. Only awe of God is capable of keeping work in its rightful place. Let me explain.

I want to repeat something I said earlier in this book because it is central to what we are talking about right now. In this book, we have focused on a theology of awe, and here's how that theology relates to you. Good theology doesn't just define who God is; it also defines who we are as his children. It's not just that God is in every way awesome in glory, but that *he is all that he is for you by grace*! God's awesome glory has been showered down on you and me by grace. He is awesome in power for us. He is awesome in sovereignty for us. He is awesome in mercy for us. He is awesome in wisdom for us. He is awesome in love for us. He is awesome in holiness for us. He is awesome in patience for us. He is awesome in faithfulness for us. He is awesome in grace for us. What he is, he is for us!

So the grace that has connected me to him has also freed me from looking for identity anywhere else. I am what I am because of who he is for me by grace. In his awesome glory, I really do find everything I need. I do not have to look elsewhere for the spiritual resources I need for living. I do not have to hunt elsewhere for meaning and purpose for my life. I do not have to look elsewhere to define who I am. I do not have to look elsewhere to measure my potential. I do not have to look elsewhere to find that inner sense of peace and well-being. Why? Because I have found all those things in him. Awe of him liberates me from a life-distorting bondage to awe of anything else. Remember, you and I tend to be in awe of what we are convinced will give us life (identity, meaning, purpose, pleasure, etc.).

So awe amnesia will leave you with an identity vacuum that you will fill with something in your life. If you forget who God is (i.e., you misdirect your awe), you will not know who you are as his child (i.e., you will lose your identity), and you will look horizontally for what you have already been given vertically. Now here's the application to the topic of this chapter: because work is such a huge and significant dimension of our lives, it becomes very tempting for us to look for our identity there. And when you look to work for your identity, you will find it very hard to resist its challenges, demands, and promises of reward.

The Horizontal Identities of Work

1. Identity in achievement/success. "I am what I have accomplished" is a very tempting place to look for identity. Success makes you feel able and competent. A trail of achievement seems to make a statement about who you are and what you are able to do. We generally celebrate successful people as our personal and cultural heroes. We tend to see success as always a good thing. But when success becomes your personal savior—that is, the place where you are looking for life—it becomes very hard to harness your drive for it. If you look to achievement to feel good about your life, to feel secure, or to have a life of meaning and purpose, then you will be dissatisfied with today's success. The buzz of today's success will fade, and you'll need the next success to keep you going and another success to follow it. You will be looking incessantly for the next mountain to conquer. Without realizing it, success will have morphed from something you enjoyed to something you cannot live without. Your heart that once desired success will now become ruled by it. Because of this, you will tend to go where success leads you, willing to invest whatever time, energy, and relationships you need to invest to get it.

Here's where it all gets dangerous. Here's where you begin to steal time away from your family, spiritual, and church commitments to get another step closer to the success that now rules your heart. I have spent lots of time with guilt-ridden absentee mothers and fathers who were driven by success and are now looking back with a huge burden of regret. I have talked with many men who sacrificed their marriages on the altar of success. I have talked with many people who still call themselves Christians but have an occasional Sunday-morning relationship with their faith because they worshiped every day at the throne of another god called achievement. Only when awe of God has redefined you as his child and given you a lasting and secure identity will you be able to keep something like a natural hunger for success in its proper place.

2. *Identity in power/control.* "I am in control; therefore, I am" is a seductive place to look for identity. In a world where most of us have so little control and where our lives often seem

out of control, control is a very powerful thing. In a world where most of us have a variety of people who tell us what to do every day, it is intoxicating to be the person in power, the one doing the commanding. In a world where you rarely know what is coming around the corner, it is tempting to see the "good life" as predictable and controlled. So how do you assure yourself that you will have the good life? The answer is easy: by working yourself into a position of power over people and things.

But identity in self-sovereignty is a dangerous thing. A wife finds no comfort in being ruled by a power-hungry, controlling husband. What she really wants is a husband who loves her. She will be comfortable in his leadership if it is an expression of servant love. Children aren't drawn to a dad who gives more rules than affection. They don't find comfort in a father who is demanding, critical, or always needing to be right because he always needs to be in control. The children of this kind of dad don't feel loved; they feel used. They feel that what their father does is done for him, not for their good. Workers never develop an appreciative loyalty toward a power-hungry boss. They will resent his constant, success-driven demands. They will hate the fact that no achievement is ever enough. No pastor is ever thankful to have a power-hungry, controlling, success-driven person as a member of his leadership team. That person will always end up creating needless conflict and division.

People who have attached their identity to success always leave a trail of personal and spiritual carnage behind them. On the contrary, awe of God teaches me that my life is under perfect control and that One of inestimable power rules all the things that I would otherwise want to rule in order to feel secure. Power and control are miserable places to find identity, yet since my life of work is a place to establish power and control, it is very hard not to work more than I should just to get them.

3. Identity in affluence/possessions. "I am the size of the pile of stuff I have accumulated" is a dangerous place to look for identity. What are the cultural markers of success and, therefore, the markers of identity? When we picture the successful person, don't we think of the big, beautiful house (lavishly furnished, of course), the luxury cars (you've got to have more than one), the expensive wardrobe, and the fine watches and jewelry? These are the images of success that the media puts before us every day. And because we are physical people living in a physical world, and because God has given us the capacity to recognize and enjoy beauty, it is tempting to identify the "good life" as a life filled with beautiful things. Now again, the desire for beautiful things is not evil in itself. In fact, when I appreciate beauty, I mirror the Creator, whose artistic hand is the source of everything beautiful. I am designed to appreciate beautiful things, but I must not attach my identity to how many of those things I possess, and I must not let my heart be ruled by them.

If you've attached your identity to material possessions and physical affluence, you will spend the bulk of your waking hours seeking to gain them, maintain them, use them, enjoy them, and keep them. And because you are constantly working to increase and maintain your pile of stuff, other areas of your life will suffer. You may have a beautiful house, but you will never have time to enjoy it, and your family will generally dwell there without you. You may have an amazing car, but that car will seldom transport you to your church to participate in its many ministries, because you just won't have the time. You will tend to live in debt, because your desire for the next thing will always exceed the size of your paycheck. Looking to physical possessions to give you identity is potentially destructive. Only when you are living in awe of the One who created and owns everything will you be able to rest as his child in the knowledge that he will faithfully provide every good thing that you need. And only when your heart is satisfied in him can you be freed from looking for spiritual satisfaction in the fleeting pleasures of the physical world. When you're satisfied in him, you will be liberated from working constantly in order to possess more of what you hope will give you identity.

Universal Temptations

It's important to humbly admit that all these things tempt us. I know they tempt me. I tend to be driven and tend to take too much personal credit for my achievements. I forget that every achievement points to God's awesome glory. I could not achieve anything without the body that he has given me, the gifts he has bestowed upon me, the control he has over me and my world, and the grace that daily rescues me from me. My successes should depend on my awe of him rather than tempting me to be in awe of me.

I wish I could say that I don't like power or don't enjoy being in control. I wish I could say that I don't need to be right or have the last word. I wish I could say that I am okay when my life is chaotic, when unexpected things enter my door, or when control over a situation is ripped out of my hands. I wish I could say that I never wonder what God is doing and always trust him when life makes no sense. I wish I could say that I find more joy in being a servant than in being the decision maker. I wish self-sacrificing love was always a greater treasure to me than ruling the day and having my say. I wish I could say all these things, but I can't. As I near the end of this book, I am deeply aware that all the battles of awe described in it rage on in my heart. I become an awe amnesiac, and when I do, I tend to work way too hard at trying to get from the people, situations, and things around me what I can only get from the God of awesome glory, who is my Savior.

I would like to think that I have set the world of physical things in its proper place, but that is not always the case. There are still times when I eat too much, spend too much, covet what someone else has, or wish that I made more so I could spend more on what my eyes are able to see and my heart is tempted to crave. Yes, I am a lot better at saying no to myself than I once was. And I know that it never works to look for spiritual heart satisfaction in physical things. But the temptation remains, and my heart is still susceptible to it.

As I have stated before, my problem is not that I live in a world awash in physical beauty. My problem is not that I have been wired to recognize and delight in that beauty. No, my problem is that when my heart is not taking in and being satisfied by the awesome beauty of my Lord, I will look for beauty elsewhere to satisfy me. Remember, every beautiful physical thing has been designed by God to point you to the incomparable beauty found in him. You see, when I don't let awe of God give my heart rest and define me as his child, I will seek identity in things like success and achievement, power and control, and possessions and affluence, and I will work like crazy to get them, leaving a trail of relational and spiritual destruction behind me.

Workaholism is not a need problem. It's not a schedule problem, a gift problem, or an opportunity problem. It happens when the awe of God is replaced by the awe of something else. When I forget that God in all his awesome glory is all that he is for me by grace, I will look for life somewhere other than in him.

What the Awe of God Teaches You about Your Work

When you require yourself to gaze upon and consider God's awesome glory, it will teach you things that will help you put your work in its proper place.

1. *The gifts that you employ in your work come from and belong to God.* Work is not about applying your abilities to achieve the life you have always dreamed of. Such an approach to work is scarily self-focused. Awe of God teaches you that work is the regular place where God calls you to be a good steward of the gifts, opportunities, and abilities he has given you. Since God has given you these gifts, you need to exercise them in submission to his will and for the sake of his glory. So how can you use these gifts in your work in a way that recognizes God as the giver and submits to the commands, values, and principles of his Word?

2. *The time that you invest in work belongs to the Lord.* I must recognize that God, in his awesome glory, is the only being in the universe who exists in timelessness. He has created me to live in and for a certain time and place. I must do all he has called me to do within the limits of the time he has given me. Since my time belongs to him, I have to live with the awareness that if my world of work expands, it will expand into the space already occupied by other things to which God has called me. I must then be careful to invest my time in a way that recognizes him and submits to all he has called me to do.

3. *You are called to live for something bigger than yourself.* Awe of God teaches me that my life is enormously bigger than merely my life. By grace, God has connected me to things that are huge and eternal. I am not at the center of things. What I want should not be the principal motivator of what I do and how I spend my time. The choices and investment I make in my world of work must always submit to the reality that I have been called to the building of a kingdom that is not my own. Success is not about how well I've been able to build my own little kingdom but about the degree to which I've done all I've done in the service of a greater King.

4. Success is not about accruing power but about resting in God's power. The most successful person is the person who knows his place. The most successful person is the person who humbly submits all that she has and all that she does to the power of One greater than her. Success is not about using my world of work to create personal power and control. Success is about recognizing God's control and using my gifts for his purpose, accepting the power that comes my way as a stewardship from him. Success also means recognizing that whatever power I have is not independent power to use however I wish to use it. All human power is representative power. God grants me this power and calls me to use it in a way that is consistent with values that he makes clear in his Word.

5. God is too wise and loving ever to call you to one area of responsibility that will necessitate you being irresponsible in another. Awe teaches me that I can never blame God for the consequences of my bad choices. God will never call me to a work life that makes biblical commitments to my family and my church impossible. If it seems impossible for me to balance my life of work with doing what God calls me to do in my family and church life, I am in the situation not because God's calls are unmanageable but because I am seeking to get things out of work that I should not. And when I do that, I will work too much and too long, and other places in my life will suffer.

6. By grace, God welcomes you to rest in the knowledge that you will find everything you need in him. Awe of God teaches me that, by grace, my life of work can now be an expression of rest and not worry. Rather than your life of work being driven by "I've got to have _____," it can now be shaped by "Look at the amazing things I have been given." Rather than work being driven by anxious need, it can now be shaped by worshipful gratitude. Yes, you are committed to work because God calls you to labor, but as you work, you can rest in his covenantal commitment to meet every one of your needs.

Many of our work lives are out of whack, so it is important for us to remember that this is not a priorities problem but an awe problem. Celebrate that you are not in this battle by yourself. In fact, God continues to battle for us even when we don't have the sense to battle for ourselves. His grace is just that awesome.

EPILOGUE

*If I find in myself a desire which no experience in this world
can satisfy, the most probable explanation is that I was made
for another world.*

C. S. LEWIS[12]

It's deep in the heart of every human being. It wanders around
in your soul, waiting to be satisfied. It is everyone's quest and,
in this life, no one's destination. The way you deal with it will
set the course of your personal narrative. Every human being
will only ever find one place of rest, one location of final fulfillment. There and there alone will the journey end, the war be
over, and our hearts be given the rest they always wanted but
never fully had.

When that time comes, we will get it right. Then we will be
completely full, never to hunger again. Then we will experience
what we have longed for at times and in ways that we didn't
even know we were longing. Then we will be happy—no, not
with the temporary physical, emotional, relational, or situational
happiness that fades like morning fog. Then we will be happy in
a deeply contented happiness of heart, a kind of joyful contentment of soul unlike anything we have ever known before.

We will no longer be haunted by ghosts of "what ifs" and
"if onlys." Then we will not wish for what others have or la-
ment what we have missed. Then we will no longer try to satisfy

spiritual hunger with physical food. Then we will be freed from trying to calm internal restlessness with things that cause us trouble and only deepen our longing. Then we will know what we have never known before, and we will celebrate that knowledge forever.

Impressed upon my mind as I have come to the end of this book is that I have failed to state explicitly one thing that would leave this book tragically incomplete. It is a glaring and significant omission. Here it is: *awe is a longing*. Perhaps that doesn't seem too thunderous to you, but it is. The capacity for awe that God has given us fundamentally explains the endless variety of human dissatisfactions. Between the "already" of our conversion and the "not yet" of eternity, we are granted greater satisfaction, but our hearts are not at rest; the war still goes on, and we crave more.

If awe is a longing, then embedded in that longing is the cry for a destination. And if awe requires a destination, then every moment of awe in this life merely prepares us for the incalculable awe that is to come. You just can't write a book about awe and not talk about eternity. Perhaps we can find no more real and present argument for heaven than the angst that we all carry in the face of the temporary and dissatisfying awes of the present. Whether we know it or not, the awe of every human being—that desire to be amazed, blown away, moved, and satisfied—is actually a universal craving to see God face-to-face. All the awesome things in creation point me to the awesome God who created and holds them together, and his presence is the destination where my hunger will finally be satisfied. God designed this present world to stimulate awe so we would hunger for another world. On the other side, we won't need the fingers of creation pointing us to God's awesome glory because we will see that glory face-to-face and dwell in the light and heat of its sun forever and ever. We will finally stand in the actual presence of God, and we will bask in heart-satisfied awe, never to long again.

It is impossible to characterize how deep and expansive our delight in him will be. It is hard to find words that do justice to how completely satisfied we will be. Our hearts will finally have what they have always searched for, and our celebration will never end.

Yes, it is true; your capacity for awe is a longing for another world. It's a craving for what this fallen world will never give you. The awe capacity of your heart cries out every day to be enveloped by the glory of God, freed from the seductive voices of competing glories. The quest for awe is a cry for the heaven that God has guaranteed for every one of his blood-purchased children.

Awe is a longing for a place where your hunger will be satisfied. Jesus has paid for and prepared that place for you. There is no greater grace than to be invited into the presence of such glory. There is no greater grace than to have your fickle heart forgiven and finally satisfied forever and ever. Amen.

> The Spirit and the Bride say, "Come." And let the one who hears say, "Come." And let the one who is thirsty come; let the one who desires take the water of life without price. . . . He who testifies to these things says, "Surely I am coming soon." Amen. Come, Lord Jesus! (Rev. 22:17, 20)

STUDY QUESTIONS

Chapter 1: Humanity

1. Which of the situations described in the beginning of the chapter hits most closely to home for you? Explain.

2. Share about something in God's creation that amazes you.

3. Discuss the statement "Where you look for awe will shape the direction of your life" (page 19).

4. Explain why rejoicing in the awesomeness of God's creation cannot be the *stopping place* for one's heart.

5. How can someone have it all yet come up empty in the end?

Chapter 2: War

1. Discuss the idea that each of our hearts is a battleground where a war rages for control of the awe of our hearts. What biblical story most clearly depicts this reality for you? How have you seen this dynamic in your own life?

2. Summarize *awe wrongedness* (AWN) in one or two sentences.

3. Consider the fact that we all struggle with awe wrongedness in spite of the fact that it is morally wrong and inescapably self-destructive. Talk about some reasons for this struggle.

4. What temptations concerning awe wrongedness do leaders need to be especially aware of?

5. Describe what the opposite of awe wrongedness looks like in general. What would it look like in a specific area of your life?

Chapter 3: Ministry

1. Read Judges 2:8–12. Though the generation under Joshua's leadership accomplished a great deal, what critical task did they fail to prioritize? See also Psalm 145:1–7.

2. What are some specific things we can remind ourselves and others of in the areas of sexuality, spending, control, and gluttony in order to avoid awe problems?

3. What heart changes need to take place in order for you to pray with a willingness to abandon your own plan for God's greater plan?

4. Discuss the importance of feeling small as we minister to those around us. Why can this be difficult in today's culture?

5. Explain why *familiarity* is such a danger in gospel ministry.

Chapter 4: Replacement

1. Briefly describe the principle of replacement. What lies and beliefs are found at the heart of replacement? What replaces awe of God in our hearts?

2. Compare a life lived in horizontal awe to one lived in vertical awe. Describe how this contrast has played out at various times in your life.

3. Explain why our problem is not that we live in a world of awe-inspiring things.

4. Why are we powerless to free ourselves from the problem of awe replacement?

5. What role does humility play in being delivered from the human pattern of awe replacement and self-slavery? Share a time when you were humbly able to celebrate the good news of God's grace.

Chapter 5: Amnesia

1. Explain the statement "Every beautiful and amazing sight, sound, color, texture, taste, and touch of the created world has glory-scopic intention built into it" (page 66).

2. Discuss which of the symptoms of blind amnesia you struggle with most frequently and why.

3. For what thing/pursuit have you judged the love of God or others by their willingness to deliver that thing/pursuit to you?

4. Do any of the listed symptoms of blind amnesia appear in your life? Explain.

5. Set aside time this week before the Savior for humble confession of your awe amnesia and failure to see and remember what the world points us to; then see what the Lord will do through his glorious grace.

Chapter 6: Transgression

1. Discuss how an awe problem produces a law problem.

2. What is shocking to you about the awe-replacement scene in the garden of Eden? In what ways are we similar to Eve?

3. What events ensue when people lose their awe of God?

4. Why is it important for our awe to be recharged? In what ways does gathered worship give people their awe back again? Share a time when you experienced a recharging of awe in your life.

5. What role do theology and rules play in having a heart filled with awe for God? What is their ultimate purpose?

Chapter 7: Complaint

1. Discuss the statement "Complaint is awelessness verbalized." How did the people of Israel verbalize their awelessness in Deuteronomy 1? How did Moses verbalize his awe?

2. What shapes your perspective on your circumstances? Share a time when your functional theology differed from your formal theology.

3. Describe the deadly outcomes of falling into a pattern of questioning God's goodness or doubting his promises.

4. How can we have hope and peace of mind in the face of our weaknesses and inabilities and in circumstances that are outside our control?

5. What will you do differently the next time you feel the urge to voice a complaint?

Chapter 8: Materialism

1. Discuss ways in which material things can "eat up our lives" (page 108).

2. Where do you tend to look for life?

3. Talk about whether it is possible for physical things to have an appropriate place in our lives—that is, how can we keep the pleasures of the material world in their proper place?

4. What is the purpose of remembrance awe? Talk about the danger of stopping at remembrance awe without allowing it to stimulate worship awe.

5. Describe ways in which God's grace encourages you even in your weakness.

Chapter 9: Growth

1. Spend time this week considering the following: Would you describe your faith as being relegated to the "spiritual/religious" part of your life, or has it become the overarching lifestyle that gives sense and meaning to all you do? Is your Christianity more a formal religious habit or a radical new way of living? Share your thoughts.

2. Discuss the connection between sanctification and awe.

3. In what way is sin more than just doing the wrong things?

4. Since we cannot produce the fruit of the Spirit in ourselves, what hope do we have to change the motivational direction of our hearts?

5. Discuss the statement "Only when God is in his rightful place will others be in the appropriate place in my heart and life" (page 128). What does this idea have to do with the fruit of the Spirit?

Chapter 10: Worldview

1. Talk about what you most need to be reminded of from Isaiah 40. What in this passage encourages you?

2. Think of a situation in your life in which you measured the size and nearness of God by assessing your circumstances. What is the problem with this approach, and how does Isaiah 40 form a corrective?

3. Which of the symptoms of two-drawer living are you most prone to exhibit? Explain.

4. Share something you have learned in this chapter or in previous chapters that will help remind you of God's presence and glory and of an accurate worldview.

Chapter 11: Church

1. Spend time this week memorizing and meditating on Colossians 3:1–2 and 12–17.

2. Talk about what the church would look like if all God's people were involved in his redemptive work all the time.

3. Explain what it means for us to be instruments of God's grace in the lives of others. What "higher purpose" does God have for our relationships?

4. Which of the five characteristics of a radical ministry lifestyle is most evident in your life? Which is least evident? Share what

changes need to take place for these characteristics to describe your lifestyle.

5. What would it take for you to be always committed and ready to teach and admonish when God gives you the opportunity?

Chapter 12: Parenting

1. How would you describe your parenting strategy up to this point—piecemeal and reactive or guided by a big, overarching vision? Explain.

2. Of what use is the law in a child's life? What important task is the law unable to accomplish? Discuss how these facts should affect your parenting strategy.

3. What in everyday life blinds you to the awesome display of God's glory everywhere around you? Spend time this week in prayer that God would graciously open your eyes to his glory and capture your heart with his awe.

4. Share what changes need to take place as you exercise authority in the lives of your children—as you are reminded that you are the look on God's face, the tone of his voice, the touch of his hand, and his character and attitude.

5. What will you do this week to point your child to God's visible glory?

Chapter 13: Work

1. Explain why success, power, and possessions are dangerous places to look for life or find identity.

2. In what ways do you find yourself being tempted in each of these areas?

3. How can you in your work more effectively steward your God-given gifts, opportunities, time, and abilities in submission to God's will for the sake of his glory?

4. Describe success in terms of the statement "The most successful person is the person who knows his place" (page 180).

Epilogue

1. Discuss the statement "Your capacity for awe is a longing for another world" (page 185). How does this idea explain our dissatisfactions?

2. Try to describe the satisfaction that will take place when we see God face-to-face.

NOTES

1. Keith and Kristyn Getty, "Don't Let Me Lose My Wonder," on *In Christ Alone*, Getty Music, Koch Records, 2007, compact disc.

2. Albert Einstein et al., *Living Philosophies* (New York: Simon and Schuster, 1931), 6.

3. G. K. Chesterton, *Tremendous Trifles* (New York: Dodd, Mead and Company, 1910), 7.

4. John Calvin, Sermon No. 10 on 1 Corinthians, quoted in William J. Bouwsma, *John Calvin: A Sixteenth-Century Portrait* (New York: Oxford University Press, 1988), 134–35.

5. Bernice Johnson Reagon, "The Songs Are Free," interview by Bill Moyers, PBS, 1991, transcript excerpt published online November 23, 2007, http://www.pbs.org/moyers/journal/11232007/transcript2.html.

6. G. K. Chesterton, *A Short History of England* (New York: John Lane Company, 1917), 72.

7. Jonathan Swift, "Thoughts on Various Subjects," in *The Works of Dr. Jonathan Swift* (Edinburgh: A. Donaldson, 1761), 8:301.

8. Oswald Chambers, *My Utmost for His Highest*, Deluxe Christian Classics (Uhrichsville, OH: Barbour, 2000), 59.

9. John Piper, *A Hunger for God: Desiring God through Fasting and Prayer* (Wheaton, IL: Crossway, 2013), 25–26.

10. Paul David Tripp, *New Morning Mercies: A Daily Gospel Devotional* (Wheaton, IL: Crossway, 2014), Nov. 10 entry.

11. C. S. Lewis, *The Problem of Pain* (New York: Simon and Schuster, 1996), 47.

12. C. S. Lewis, *Mere Christianity* (New York: Simon and Schuster, 1996), 121.

GENERAL INDEX

achievement, and identity, 173–74
Adam and Eve: AWN of, 27–28, 54–55; disobedience of, 82–85
addiction, 60–61, 113, 126, 142
admonishing, 153
adultery, 45, 87–88; spiritual adultery, 81, 85–88
affluence, and identity, 176–77
"already" and "not yet," and the journey between them, 25–26, 44–45, 91, 113, 120–21, 127, 138, 184
"American dream," the, and Christianity, 150
anger, 19–20, 57, 72–73, 91, 126, 151–52
anxiety, 50, 113, 139, 141
atheism, of Christians, 137, 138
autonomy, lie of, 161
awe: horizontal awe, 21, 49, 60, 155; as a longing for eternity, 184–85; remembrance awe, 114–15; vertical awe, 21, 60, 69, 99, 109, 155; what awe does, 90–91; worship awe, 115. *See also* awe: helicopter view of
awe, helicopter view of: awe is everyone's lifelong pursuit, 17–18; awe stimulates the greatest joys and deepest sorrows in us all, 19–20; awesome stuff never satisfies, 21; every created awe is meant

to point you to the Creator, 20–21; God created an awesome world, 18; God created you with an awe capacity, 18–19; misplaced awe keeps us perennially dissatisfied, 20; where you look for awe will shape the direction of your life, 19
awe amnesia, 31, 44–45, 51, 60, 61, 65, 88, 91, 173, 177. *See also* blind amnesia
awe capacity, 18–19, 25–26, 154–55
awe problems: adultery, 45, 87–88; control, 32, 45, 71, 103, 141–42, 174–75; debt, 45, 113, 143, 176; fear of man, 45, 50, 143; gluttony, 45; materialism, 19, 26, 45, 107–8, 112–13, 143, 176–77; obesity, 45, 113; power, 45, 51, 174–75. *See also* awe problems, principles of
awe problems, principles of: awe amnesia always leads to awe replacement, 60; only grace can give us back our awe of God again, 61–64; we quickly replace awe of God with awe of self, 61; we replace vertical awe with horizontal addiction, 60–61; your emotional life is always a window into

praise, 98
prayer, and AWN, 47
pride, 26, 49

Reagon, Bernice Johnson, 79
reconciliation, 124; reconciliation
    of justification, 124; reconcilia-
    tion of sanctification, 124
relationships: the consequences of
    a personal-happiness agenda
    for relationships, 151–52; as
    a dimension of one's calling,
    171; the qualities God expects
    believers to nurture in relation-
    ships, 151, 152; relational
    dysfunction, 70–71
respect, of others, 26
rest, 103, 142; resting in God's
    covenantal commitment to
    meet every one of your needs,
    180–81; resting in God's
    power, 180; resting in the
    peace of Christ, 152
rivalry, 126
running away, 104

Sabbath, the, 90
sanctification, 121, 123, 129; the
    reconciliation of sanctification,
    124
Saul, disobedience of, 34–35
self-assuredness, 49
self-centeredness, 69
self-sufficiency, lie of, 161–62
sexual immorality, 123. *See also*
    adultery
sin, 26, 55–56, 62, 112, 124, 126;
    what sin does (makes us all
    lawbreakers and awe break-
    ers), 121–23, 126
spiritual adultery, 81, 85–88
spiritual blindness, 164, 165
spiritual coldness, 75
spiritual growth. *See* sanctification
strife, 126

success: and identity, 173–74; as
    not about accruing power but
    about resting in God's power,
    180
Swift, Jonathan, 107

teaching, 153
temptation, 55, 84, 85; universal
    temptations, 177–78
Ten Commandments, the, 88–91;
    essential order of, 89; the
    fourth commandment as a gift
    of grace, 90
theology: influence of on our
    daily living, 99–100; as a lens
    through which you examine
    life, 99; purpose of, 92
timidity, 104
"total involvement paradigm,"
    151
transgression. *See* disobedience
"two-drawer" living, 135–36,
    138–39; as more natural to us,
    139–40; the real-life drawer,
    135, 139; the spiritual-life
    drawer, 135–36, 139. *See also*
    "two-drawer" living, signs of.
"two-drawer" living, signs of,
    140–41; addiction, 60–61,
    113, 126, 142; anxiety, 50,
    113, 139, 141; control, 32,
    45, 71, 103, 141–42, 174–75;
    debt, 45, 113, 143, 176;
    depression, 57–58, 142–43;
    dissatisfaction, 16, 20, 144;
    fear of man, 45, 50, 143;
    workaholism, 51, 143–44,
    170–71, 178

vengeance, 59

wisdom: autonomous wisdom, 85;
    God as Wisdom, 85
work: as a dimension of one's
    calling, 171; and identity,

172–73; and the limits of time, 170–72; and universal temptations, 177–78. *See also* work, horizontal identities of; work, what the awe of God teaches you about it

work, horizontal identities of: identity in achievement/success, 173–74; identity in affluence/possessions, 176–77; identity in power/control, 174–75

work, what the awe of God teaches you about it: by grace, God welcomes you to rest in the knowledge that you will find everything you need in him, 180–81; the gifts that you employ in your work come from and belong to God, 179; God is too wise and loving ever to call you to one area of responsibility that will necessitate you being irresponsible in another, 180; success is not about accruing power but about rest-

ing in God's power, 180; the time that you invest in work belongs to God, 179; you are called to live for something bigger than yourself, 179

workaholism, 51, 143–44, 170–71, 178

world, the: as awesome, 18, 20–21; as designed to point us to God, 20–21, 114–15, 163; as a gloryscape, 66–67, 76, 163, 164–65; as God's good gift to us, 111; as mnemonic, 67–68, 76; as pleasurable, 111–12; the proper relationship to the physical world, 111; as a reminder of God, 114

worry, 32, 113

worship, 75; AWN in acts of worship, 29; in the first four commandments, 89–90; and reservation of the Sabbath to God, 90; worship awe, 90–91, 113

SCRIPTURE INDEX

 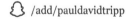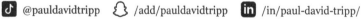

Also Available from Paul David Tripp

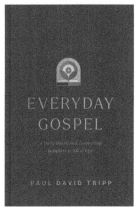

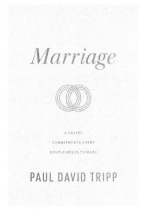

For more information, visit
crossway.org or **paultripp.com**.